When

Finds Its Song Again

Book Two: Whispers of

My Heart Series

Forty Days of Faith, Reflection, and Renewal

By

C. Pointer Benton

Published by: Self-Publish
Printed in the United States of America

First Edition

Acknowledgments

This devotional is the result of many prayers, encouragements, and gentle nudges from the people God has placed in my life. I am deeply thankful to my family, friends, and church community, who constantly remind me that God restores, renews, and teaches our hearts to sing again.

To my mentors and teachers of faith, thank you for modeling a life anchored in devotion, discipline, and unwavering trust. Your examples continue to guide my steps.

To every reader and fellow pilgrim on this journey, thank you for walking through these forty days with me. Your openness to reflect, listen, and lean into God's presence is a sacred gift.

Most of all, I give thanks to God, the Father, the Son, and the Holy Spirit, who keeps writing melodies of grace into my life and calling my heart back to His.

Table of Contents

Preface

When I first began writing this devotional, it grew out of a deep longing for my own heart to find its song again in the midst of ordinary days and challenging seasons. Lent has always been, for me, a sacred time of searching, surrender, and quiet reflection. It is a season where God gently rewrites the melodies we thought were lost and restores hope in places we thought had grown silent.

Through grief and through joy, I have discovered that God continues to offer the same invitation: to return, to listen, to come closer. This devotional was not written from a place of perfection, but from a heart learning daily what it means to walk with Christ and to trust the music He is composing within me.

My prayer is that as you journey through these forty days, you will find space to breathe, to listen, and to rest in God's presence. May these reflections, prayers, hymns, and spiritual practices help quiet the noise around you and open your heart to the One who meets you with compassion in every moment.

I invite you to walk slowly through these pages. Let the Scriptures speak deeply. Let the prayers guide your posture. Let the hymns steady your spirit. Most of all, let this be a journey toward the God who loves you without measure and is always welcoming your heart back into His song.

With gratitude and hope,
C. Pointer Benton

Introduction:
A Journey of Returning

The Lenten season is one of the Church's most sacred invitations, a call to return.

For forty days (not counting Sundays), we are asked to slow down and reflect, to lay aside the distractions that consume us and draw near to the heart of God. It is a time of repentance, but not of shame. A time of sacrifice, but not of deprivation. Lent is a sacred journey of the soul, one that leads us from ashes to resurrection, from wilderness wandering to the empty tomb.

Historically, Lent mirrors the forty days Jesus spent fasting in the wilderness, preparing for His public ministry. In that quiet place of testing and communion, Jesus was strengthened. In that same spirit, we enter these days not merely to give something up, but to make space for something far greater: the presence of God.

The Purpose of This Devotional

This devotional is designed to walk with you gently through the season of Lent. Each Monday through Saturday includes:

- A guiding Scripture to center your thoughts
- A Reflection to stir your heart and awaken your spirit
- A simple Pause and Practice to ground the reading in your daily life
- A sacred Hymn suggestion for deeper meditation and worship

Sundays, which traditionally celebrate resurrection, are intentionally left open for worship, rest, and reflection.

You may choose to read each day's entry in the morning to shape your heart for the day ahead, or in the evening as a way to wind down and reconnect with what matters most. There's no wrong way, only the way that helps you return.

Week 1:
Turning Toward God

Day 1 - Return

Scripture: Joel 2:12 – *"Even now," declares the Lord, "return to me with all your heart."*

Reflection:

Lent begins not with shame, but with a divine welcome. The season is not defined by guilt or condemnation, but by an invitation from God to return. "Even now," declares the Lord; even now, after distractions, after distance, after spiritual drought, and even after seasons of wandering, you are still invited to come back. It doesn't matter how far you've drifted, how much time has passed, or how broken you may feel. God's invitation stands firm: "Return to me with all your heart." It's a call to come as we are, without pretense, without needing to have everything perfect, but simply offering our hearts in surrender.

In this moment, God doesn't wait for us to become perfect before He embraces us; He desires our presence. Perfection is not the goal; intimacy with Him is. The act of returning to God is sacred. It's not about fixing every part of our lives before we come to Him; it's about stepping out of our own stories and into His embrace. It is the simple, powerful choice to turn toward Him, acknowledging that we need His help and His love. This isn't about doing more or trying harder; it's about offering our hearts to God, exactly where they are, and trusting that His love will meet us in the mess.

In a world that demands performance, where our worth is often measured by what we accomplish, Lent reminds us of grace. There is no checklist to earn God's love; only the courage to turn toward it. God's love doesn't come with conditions. His grace is a gift, not a reward for good behavior or flawless living. It's an invitation to let go of the pressure to perform and simply trust in His goodness.

Lent is not just about what you give up; it's about what you take in, the grace of God, the presence of Christ, and the invitation to return. Let today mark the moment your heart says "yes" to the journey home. It is a return to God with all of who you are, your fears, your doubts, your hopes, and your hurts. There's no need to hold back. God is calling you to bring everything to Him, and He promises to meet you with mercy and love.

In this season, let go of striving for perfection and embrace the love that comes freely from God. As you return to Him, know that His arms are wide open, waiting to restore and renew you. The journey of Lent is not about proving something to God, but about drawing nearer to Him and allowing His grace to transform your heart.

Pause and Practice:
Quietly say, Lord, I return to You, and sit in silence for 2 minutes. Feel the warmth of divine welcome.

Listen: "Softly and Tenderly Jesus Is Calling"

Day 2 - Silence

Scripture: Psalm 62:1 – *"Truly my soul finds rest in God; my salvation comes from him."*

Reflection:

Silence can be awkward. In a world filled with noise, whether from our devices, our schedules, or our own internal chatter, silence often feels uncomfortable, even unsettling. Yet, it is in these quiet spaces that God often speaks the loudest. Silence is where the soul can truly find rest, where the weight of the world falls away, and we can hear the still, small voice of the Creator. In our constantly connected lives, it takes real courage to unplug, to step away from the constant stream of information, and to simply be still. But this stillness is not empty; it is full of God's presence, waiting to fill the void.

When we embrace silence, we allow our souls to catch up with our bodies. In the hustle and bustle of daily life, it's easy to get disconnected from the deep parts of ourselves. Our minds race, our hearts are pulled in a thousand directions, and we lose touch with the stillness that our spirits crave. But silence creates a sacred space for us to breathe again, to recalibrate, and to reconnect with the very core of who we are. It is in the quiet that we find a profound rest, not just physical rest, but spiritual renewal.

As we sit in silence, distractions begin to fall away. The noise in our heads, the worries, the fears, the to-do lists, all of it starts to still. And in that stillness, we begin to hear more clearly. We hear our own longings, our own desires, and beneath them, we hear the whisper of God calling us back to Himself. He isn't hiding from us in the silence; He is waiting patiently for us to notice Him. In the chaos of life, we often overlook God's voice, but in the quiet, we can begin to recognize that He has been there all along, waiting to speak into our hearts.

Lent is an invitation to step away from the noise, to find the courage to be still, and to listen once again. It's a season where we can intentionally make space for God to speak, to guide, and to renew us. Just as Psalm 62:1 reminds us, "Truly my soul finds rest in God," we are invited to rest in His presence, to find peace in the quiet, and to allow His voice to soothe and strengthen us.

In this season of Lent, take the time to embrace silence, not as an uncomfortable void, but as a space filled with the presence of God. Allow the distractions to fall away and listen for His whisper. In the silence, you will find the rest your soul craves. God is waiting to meet you there. Let this Lent be a time where you step away from the noise and rediscover the deep peace that comes from resting in His presence.

Pause and Practice:
Take 5 minutes with no phone, music, or noise. Sit in God's presence. Ask, What are You saying, Lord?

Listen: "Be Still My Soul"

Day 3 - Hunger

Scripture: Matthew 5:6 – *"Blessed are those who hunger and thirst for righteousness, for they will be filled."*

Reflection:

We all know the feeling of hunger, the physical pangs in our stomachs reminding us that we need sustenance. We hunger for food, for love, for meaning, and for connection. But beneath every craving, whether for tangible things or deeper desires, there lies a spiritual hunger, a longing that only God can truly satisfy. This hunger goes beyond the surface needs of our daily lives; it speaks to a deeper yearning for purpose, for peace, and for the righteousness that only God can provide. Jesus, in His Beatitudes, doesn't shame hunger. He doesn't criticize it or condemn it as something to be avoided. Instead, He blesses it. He calls those who hunger and thirst for righteousness blessed because He knows that in their longing, they are opening themselves to the only One who can fill them.

Jesus turns our cravings, our spiritual thirsts and desires, into an invitation to be filled. The ache we experience in our hearts is not something to run from or suppress. It's an invitation to come closer to God. When we feel a deep longing for clarity, connection, or peace, we are being invited to bring that hunger to God. It's in these moments of yearning that we are most open to His presence. Instead of filling the void with distractions or fleeting pleasures, we are called to surrender those longings to Him, trusting that He is the only one who can satisfy them.

Lent is not about starving ourselves physically or emotionally; it's about awakening the holy longing in our souls. The season calls us to turn our desires, our hunger, and our thirst toward God. It's about recognizing that every ache we feel, whether for a deeper connection, a sense of direction, or inner peace, is a sacred call to draw closer to Him. The hunger we experience is not something to be ignored or suppressed, but something to be embraced as part of our spiritual journey.

Let that hunger pull you deeper into prayer. When you feel the yearning for more, more understanding, more intimacy with God, more wholeness, see it as a sacred offering, a recognition of your need for Him. In the quiet longing, God meets us. In our thirst, He satisfies. During Lent, we are invited to step away from the distractions that try to fill the space in our hearts and allow God's presence to fill us instead. Through this process of surrender, we open ourselves to receive the righteousness that only God can give, a righteousness that brings peace, clarity, and an abundant life.

So today, as you experience hunger, in whatever form it takes, view it as a moment of divine invitation. Let that longing guide you back to God, and trust that He will fill you with all you need. Lent is not about deprivation; it is about awakening to the deeper hunger of the soul and allowing God to fill it with His love, His truth, and His righteousness.

Pause and Practice:
When hunger rises, literal or emotional, pause and say, Lord, fill me with what I truly need.

Listen: "Fill My Cup, Lord"

Day 4 – Stillness

Scripture: Psalm 46:10 – *"Be still, and know that I am God."*

Reflection:

Stillness isn't just about stopping your body; it's about calming your soul. In our fast-paced world, we are often caught up in a cycle of rushing, striving, and juggling responsibilities. We are taught to go, do, achieve, and produce, and we fear what might surface when we pause. What will we face if we stop moving for just a moment? What discomfort, uncertainty, or emotions might rise? But stillness is not an absence of action; it is a space of holy presence where God meets us. It's the opportunity to move beyond doing and to simply be in the presence of the One who holds all things together.

Psalm 46:10 invites us into that holy stillness: "Be still, and know that I am God." In this stillness, we stop performing, stop trying to prove ourselves, and stop striving to control the outcomes. Instead, we open ourselves to receive what God wants to offer us, His peace, His assurance, His presence. The truth that emerges in stillness is that we are not the ones holding everything together; God is. This pause is not a time of emptiness, but a time of sacred rest. It's when we surrender the illusion of control and recognize our complete dependence on God.

In that space of stillness, God's voice speaks clearly: "I've got you." In the chaos of our lives, we can easily forget that God is in control, that He holds the world—and us—in His hands. The fear of stopping can be overwhelming because it forces us to confront our vulnerabilities and our need for Him. But when we take the time to be still, we acknowledge that we are not self-sufficient, and we allow ourselves to hear God's comforting, unwavering promise: "I've got you." Sometimes, that is all we need to hear, everything else fades into the background when we rest in the truth that God is present with us, guiding us, and sustaining us.

Lent calls us into this more profound stillness. It's not about doing more or accomplishing a list of tasks. It's about creating space to sit quietly in God's presence, letting go of the noise, and allowing Him to fill the silence with His love and peace. This stillness invites us to release our anxiety, to stop striving, and to trust that in His presence, we are enough. We don't have to do anything to earn His love; we just need to be with Him.

Today, let the stillness be a reminder of who God is and who you are in Him. Allow your soul to rest in His embrace, knowing that He is God, and He is in control. When you feel overwhelmed or tempted to rush, remember that stillness is not the absence of movement; it is the gift of holy presence, where God whispers, "I've got you." In that moment, we find everything we need.

Pause and Practice:
Sit in stillness. Place your hand over your heart. Breathe. Whisper, I am still, and You are God.

Listen: "Near to the Heart of God"

Day 5 - Begin

Scripture: Isaiah 43:19 – *"See, I am doing a new thing! Now it springs up; do you not perceive it?"*

Reflection:

Lent is a fresh beginning, not a punishment. It is not a season of self-inflicted guilt or striving to earn something from God, but a time of profound renewal, a chance for your soul to hit the reset button. Often, we feel like we're behind, like we've missed our opportunity for change or growth. But Lent reminds us that we are precisely where grace finds us, no earlier, no later. God doesn't measure our progress by human standards of success or productivity; He meets us right where we are, with fresh mercy and the opportunity for transformation. God is doing something new, not just in the world, but in you.

The beauty of this season is that it invites us into the possibility of newness, not through our own efforts but through the grace of God. It's easy to dismiss the small beginnings, the quiet stirrings in our hearts, thinking they aren't significant enough to make an impact. But just as a seed doesn't question whether it will become a tree, we must trust that God is working in the hidden places. Growth doesn't always happen in dramatic moments or grand gestures; it occurs in the quiet, unseen spaces where God nurtures and cultivates life within us. Small starts are the foundation for something much larger. Trust the process and trust that God is at work in every small step.

Lent calls us to embrace the new thing God is doing within us. It's not about striving harder or trying to create change on our own, it's about surrendering to the transformation God wants to bring. The work of renewal in our hearts and lives is not something we can create or force. It's something we receive. The invitation is not to earn newness, but to receive it as a gift. Newness is not something you create; it's something you accept.

As you step into this season, let today be your yes to the new thing God is doing. Open your heart to His work, even if it starts small or doesn't look like what you expected. The process of renewal often begins in hidden places, beneath the surface, and unfolds over time. Trust that God is bringing forth something beautiful in your life, even if you can't fully see it yet. Allow yourself to let go of the need to control or understand everything. Surrender to His timing, knowing that He is faithful to bring about the growth and change He promises.

Lent is an invitation to step into God's newness with open hands. You are not behind; you are right where you need to be, and God is at work in you. Let your soul rest in the assurance that, as you surrender, God will bring forth the new thing He has for you, growing you in ways that only He can.

Pause and Practice:
Pray: God, I welcome the new thing You're doing in me. Help me begin again today.

Listen: "Great Is Thy Faithfulness"

Day 6 - Trust

Scripture: Proverbs 3:5 – *"Trust in the Lord with all your heart and lean not on your own understanding."*

Reflection:

To trust God is to let go of the outcome. It's a conscious decision to place our confidence not in our ability to control, but in His ability to lead. Trust is a powerful act of surrender, an acknowledgment that we cannot foresee or understand every twist and turn of life's journey. It is choosing peace even when answers don't come quickly, when clarity is elusive, and when the road ahead is uncertain. Trusting in God doesn't mean we have all the answers, it means we have faith in the One who holds all the answers, even when we can't see them ourselves.

Trust doesn't always feel certain. In fact, it often feels like a step into the unknown. It feels vulnerable to let go of the tight grip we have on our circumstances and our plans. Trust isn't a guarantee of comfort; it's a surrender of control. It's not about blindly following, but about leaning into a relationship with God, rooted in His character and His promises. Our trust is anchored in the knowledge that God is good, faithful, and loving. It's rooted in the relationship we have with Him, the deep awareness that He is with us in every moment, guiding us with His wisdom and grace.

When you trust God, you admit your limits. You recognize that you don't have the answers and that you can't control every outcome. But in this admission, you embrace God's limitless grace. Our understanding, our limitations, or our shortcomings do not bind his grace. His grace covers us in our weakness, offering strength when we feel depleted, clarity when we feel confused, and hope when we feel lost. Trusting in God means releasing the need to figure everything out on your own. You don't have to understand everything today; you only need to lean in.

In that leaning, in that act of surrender, strength is found. Strength is not found in our ability to have all the answers or to control every situation, it is found in holding onto the One who does. God's wisdom, knowledge, and power are infinite, and when we trust Him, we align ourselves with His unshakable strength. He is the anchor that holds us steady in the storms of life. When we lean not on our own understanding but on His, we find peace during uncertainty and grace in the midst of struggle.

Today, take a moment to reflect on where you need to trust God more fully. What areas of your life have you been trying to control or figure out on your own? Choose to let go of the outcome and surrender those things to God. Trust that He will guide you, that He will provide for you, and that His grace is more than enough for every situation. Remember, it's not about having all the answers, it's about leaning into the One who does. Let go, trust Him, and find strength in His faithful presence.

Pause and Practice:
Name one thing you've been trying to control. Whisper, God, I trust You with this.

Listen: "Tis So Sweet to Trust in Jesus"

Week 2:
Inner Work

Day 7 - Repent

Scripture: Acts 3:19 – *"Repent, then, and turn to God, so that your sins may be wiped out, that times of refreshing may come from the Lord."*

Reflection:

Repentance isn't about shame or self-condemnation, it's about coming clean before the One who already knows every part of our story and still loves us unconditionally. Often, we associate repentance with guilt and fear of punishment, but the true essence of repentance is not about shame; it's about healing, renewal, and restoration. To repent is to acknowledge that something in our lives isn't working, that we've strayed from the path God intended for us, and it's an invitation to change direction. It's a turning away from the things that hinder us and a turning back to the God who is always waiting to receive us with open arms.

Repentance is an act of grace, not an act of punishment. God doesn't use repentance as a tool for condemnation; He uses it as a pathway to heal. When we repent, we bring our brokenness and our failings into the light, and God, in His mercy, wipes them away. In that act of turning back to Him, we are not met with judgment, but with mercy. It is through repentance that we experience God's forgiveness, and in that forgiveness, we find peace and restoration. It's not about dwelling in our mistakes, but about trusting that God is bigger than our failures and that He desires to restore us to wholeness.

Repentance opens the door to refreshment. In the act of returning to God, there is a sense of renewal, a fresh breath of grace that washes over us, giving us the strength to move forward. The weight of guilt is lifted, and in its place, we receive God's love, peace, and the refreshing power of His Holy Spirit. Times of refreshing come from the Lord when we are honest with Him and allow His grace to renew our hearts. It's a space where we can breathe again, where the heaviness of sin and shame is replaced with the lightness of His forgiveness.

God is waiting to welcome you with mercy, not judgment. Repentance is not something to fear; it is something to embrace because it is how we are restored and healed. God accepts us for our mistakes; He calls us back to Himself with open arms, ready to forgive and to renew. In the honesty of repentance, we find freedom, not just from sin, but from the weight of trying to live in our own strength, apart from God.

Today, reflect on areas of your life where you need to return to God. Repentance doesn't require perfection, it requires honesty and a willingness to change. Let today be a moment where you bring your whole self before God, acknowledging what isn't working and trusting that He will help you live differently. There is refreshment waiting for you on the other side of honesty, a new season of healing, peace, and grace. Trust that as you turn to Him, He welcomes you with mercy, not judgment.

Pause and Practice:
Ask God to reveal one area of your life where a fresh turn is needed. Whisper, Lead me, Lord.

Listen: "Just As I Am"

Day 8 - Confess

Scripture: 1 John 1:9 – *"If we confess our sins, he is faithful and just and will forgive us our sins and purify us from all unrighteousness."*

Reflection:

Confession is not just about listing wrongs; it's about releasing the heavy burden of carrying them. Too often, we weigh guilt, shame, and regret as if we are somehow responsible for bearing them. But confession offers us the freedom to lay that burden down. It's an act of honesty before God, a recognition that we need His grace, that we are not self-sufficient, and that we cannot heal ourselves. When we confess, we are agreeing with God about our brokenness and our need for His forgiveness and mercy. It is a step away from pretending to be something we're not and a step toward the freedom of being fully honest with the One who already knows our hearts.

God doesn't need our confession to learn what we've done. He already knows it all. Our confession isn't for His benefit, it's for ours. We confess to align ourselves with the truth, to acknowledge our need for Him, and to invite His healing into the areas of our lives that are still broken. God's forgiveness doesn't depend on us being perfect or on us "performing" for His approval. It's a gift of grace, freely given to those who admit their need for it.

When we confess, we stop pretending. We stop hiding behind the facade of self-sufficiency or the fear of rejection. Confession is an invitation to come as we are, knowing that God's love and forgiveness are not based on our performance but on His faithfulness. It's a moment of release, an opportunity to hand over our sins, our shame, and our guilt and to receive the forgiveness and purifying love that only God can offer.

Today is not about guilt; it's about grace. Grace flows when we open our hearts in honesty, when we allow God's love to meet us in our brokenness. The beauty of 1 John 1:9 is that it promises that God is not only faithful and just in forgiving our sins but also in purifying us from all unrighteousness. The act of confession doesn't just wipe away our wrongs; it transforms us. It restores us to a place of wholeness and purity, a place where we can walk in the freedom of God's forgiveness.

If there are areas of your life where you feel burdened by sin, guilt, or shame, take a moment to confess. Let go of the weight you've been carrying and allow God's grace to wash over you. Know that in this space of honesty and surrender, God is faithful to forgive and to purify, making you whole again. Let today be a moment of release, a step into the freedom that comes from knowing that God's grace is always available and consistently enough.

Pause and Practice:
Speak or write one confession to God. Trust His forgiveness. Receive His cleansing love.

Listen: "I Surrender All"

Day 9 - Cleanse

Scripture: Psalm 51:7 – *"Cleanse me with hyssop, and I will be clean; wash me, and I will be whiter than snow."*

Reflection:

The desire to be clean, to truly be free from the stains that mar our souls, runs deep within every person. It's not just about outward cleanliness; it's about the inner purification that our hearts long for. We all carry spiritual stains: the weight of regret for past decisions, the heavy burden of shame we can't seem to shake, or the bitterness that lingers from unhealed wounds. These invisible marks can cling to us, shaping the way we see ourselves and the world around us.

But the good news of Lent, the hope we hold onto amid our journey, is that God's grace is not a surface-level wash. It's not just about brushing off the dirt; it's about a deep, transformative cleansing. God doesn't just forgive and leave us in the same state; He cleanses us, purifies us, and makes us new. When we seek His mercy, we don't just experience a momentary relief; we are made whole.

Psalm 51 speaks of the ritual purification of the priesthood, where hyssop was used to cleanse both the body and the soul. David, who wrote this psalm in a moment of deep repentance, acknowledges his need for a cleansing far beyond what any earthly remedy could provide. His plea is not just for forgiveness, but for a thorough, soul-deep washing. And God, in His infinite mercy, promises to do just that for us.

No matter what clings to your spirit today, no matter how dark the stain or how long it's been there, God's mercy is more than enough to wash it away. The blood of Jesus reaches into every hidden corner, every shadowed place, every wound that you've kept buried. His grace is not limited by time, by the severity of your sin, or by the depth of your pain.

Perhaps today, the hardest thing for you to grasp is that you are not beyond grace, that you are not too broken to be restored. You may feel that your past mistakes, your regrets, or your fears disqualify you from God's love. But the truth is, no sin is too great, no shame too deep, for God's cleansing power.

Let Him wash you, not just from the guilt that weighs you down, but from the lies you've believed about yourself. The lies that say you are unworthy, unforgivable, or beyond repair. In Christ, you are not only forgiven, but you are also made new. He restores your identity, reshapes your heart, and calls you beloved.

Today, as you sit in God's presence, allow Him to cleanse not only the external but the internal, those places where you have believed lies, where you have held onto unforgiveness, or where you have felt unworthy of His love. He wants to wash you in His mercy, making you whiter than snow, pure, free, and wholly His. In His embrace, you are made clean. You are restored. You are whole. And that is a grace beyond measure.

Pause and Practice:
Visualize God's mercy as cleansing water. Let it wash over your heart. Say, 'Make me new, O God.'

Listen: "Nothing but the Blood of Jesus"

Day 10 - Humility

Scripture: Philippians 2:3 – *"Do nothing out of selfish ambition or vain conceit. Rather, in humility value others above yourselves."*

Reflection:

Humility is often misunderstood. It is not about diminishing ourselves or thinking less of our worth; it's about thinking of ourselves less. It's the freedom from the constant need to be right, to be noticed, or to be praised. Humility invites us to release the tight grip of ego that pushes us to be first, to be seen, or to be heard. It asks us to step back, to recognize that life isn't a race, but a journey we share with others.

Jesus is the ultimate model of humility. He, the King of the Universe, did not come to demand service but to serve. He chose the lowest place, washing the feet of His disciples, a task reserved for the lowest of servants. He embraced the cross, not for His own gain, but out of love for us. He demonstrated that true greatness comes not from power, prestige, or position, but from a heart of service.

Lent challenges us to stop climbing the ladder of self-importance and start kneeling in service to others. It teaches us that humility is not a weakness but a strength, a strength that seeks the well-being of others, that listens with compassion, and that loves with sincerity. In moments of humility, we stop trying to assert our own desires and instead make space for the needs, stories, and struggles of those around us.

As we kneel in humility, we begin to see others more clearly, not as obstacles to our success, but as individuals worthy of love, respect, and dignity. We begin to value them above ourselves, as the Scripture calls us to do. In doing so, we are freed from the weight of selfish ambition and find joy in serving, in loving, and in giving.

In these sacred days of Lent, let us remember that we are all, ultimately, dust, fragile and finite. But we are also all beloved, equally cherished by the Creator. Humility allows us to see this truth: that we are no better, no more deserving, no more important than anyone else. We are all recipients of grace, called to extend that same grace to those around us. In embracing humility, we make space for love to flourish, for relationships to deepen, and for Christ's love to shine through our actions.

Pause and Practice:
Ask God to show you where pride might be hiding. How can you serve humbly today?

Listen: "The Servant Song"

Day 11 – Surrender

Scripture: Luke 22:42 – *"Father, if you are willing, take this cup from me; yet not my will, but yours be done."*

Reflection:

Surrender is often seen as a sign of giving up, but in truth, it is an act of profound worship and a powerful expression of faith. Jesus, in His most agonizing moment, shows us that surrender does not mean the absence of struggle, but rather the willingness to trust in God's will, even when it demands the ultimate sacrifice. As He knelt in the Garden of Gethsemane, feeling the weight of the coming cross, He poured out His heart in prayer, asking, "Father, if you are willing, take this cup from me." Jesus, fully aware of the pain, the suffering, and the separation He would face, didn't shrink from His feelings or try to escape them. He acknowledged His fear and sorrow, yet still, He prayed, "Not my will, but yours be done." In this moment, He demonstrated the heart of true surrender not in the absence of struggle, but in the presence of faith that chooses God's plan over self-preservation.

To surrender is not weakness, nor is it a passive resignation to life's circumstances. Instead, it is an active, conscious choice to lay down our will in favor of God's. Surrender is an intentional turning over of our desires, our control, and even our very plans to the One who knows far better than we do. It's a decision to trust that God's will is not only wiser but is also perfectly timed and more fulfilling than any plan we could create on our own. Jesus' prayer in the garden wasn't just an expression of submitting to an inevitable fate; it was a declaration of trust, a demonstration of complete reliance on God's sovereignty.

In our own lives, surrender often involves deep struggle. It's not about a passive giving in but an active wrestling with God, acknowledging that we have our own desires and fears, yet choosing to trust His greater purpose. It's about stepping away from our need to control and giving ourselves over to the divine plan, even when we don't fully understand it or when it leads us down a difficult path. Surrender means giving God the space to lead us, even when the road ahead seems uncertain or painful.

When we pray, "Not my will, but yours," we echo Christ's courage in Gethsemane, aligning our hearts with His. This is not a one-time prayer; it's a daily act of yielding, a continual surrender of our lives to God. Each time we say, "Your will, not mine," we step into a deeper relationship with Him, trusting that He will guide us, strengthen us, and shape us into who He's calling us to be.

True surrender also involves a release of our desire for approval, recognition, or control. It's about valuing God's purpose over our own comfort. When we surrender, we are not just letting go of control over our circumstances; we are submitting to a greater mission. This submission is not the end of our personal desires but the refinement of them, aligning them with God's will so that His work can be accomplished through us. It's a surrender that is deeply active, as it calls us to walk in faith, to move forward with courage, and to trust that God's will is always good, even when we cannot see the bigger picture.

Jesus' surrender in Gethsemane teaches us that surrender is not an easy path, but it is the way to true peace. It is the way to the fullness of God's purpose for our lives. Just as Christ's surrender led to His victory on the cross and to the salvation of the world, our surrender leads us to a life that is deeply connected to God's plan, a life of grace, trust, and transformation. Each time we choose to surrender, we are making space for God's presence to work in us and through us in powerful, redemptive ways.

Surrender is the ultimate act of faith, the deepest form of worship, and the truest expression of our trust in God. When we surrender, we are saying, "I trust You, Lord, more than I trust my own understanding." In this, we find that surrender does not take away our power; it restores it. Because in God's will, we are made whole, and in His hands, we are shaped into something far more beautiful than we could ever imagine.

Pause and Practice:
Pray, not my will, but Yours. Mean it. Let go, even if just for today.

Listen: "Have Thine Own Way, Lord"

Day 12 - Mercy

Scripture: Lamentations 3:22-23 – *"Because of the Lord's great love we are not consumed, for his compassions never fail. They are new every morning."*

Reflection:

Mercy is the quiet strength that meets us in the mess of our lives. It doesn't wait for us to get our lives together or to deserve it; it simply shows up, time and time again. Mercy is the light that breaks through the darkest nights, the warmth that greets us after a season of cold sorrow. It is the fresh start that comes each morning, not because we've earned it, but because God is faithful and full of love.

In a world where so much is uncertain and temporary, God's mercy is a constant. It doesn't grow weary or run out; it is ever-present and never fails. The very fact that we wake up each morning is a testimony to the depth of God's compassion toward us. We are not consumed by our mistakes, our struggles, or the weight of yesterday's burdens, because His mercy is new with every sunrise. Every new day, no matter how heavy the heart or uncertain the path, is a reminder that we are still loved, still called, and still held in His grace.

God's mercy is not a one-time gift, something to be hoped for only in times of desperation. It is an ongoing, daily blessing that sustains us. Like daily bread, it nourishes and strengthens us, even when we feel weak or unworthy. It isn't based on what we do or fail to do; it is rooted in who God is. His mercy flows toward us not because we've done something to earn it, but because He is a loving, merciful Father who is always faithful.

When we wake up, we are given another chance, a new opportunity to experience God's kindness and grace. It's a new beginning, a fresh page, where yesterday's regrets and failures are covered in His love. In this, we are invited to lay down our fears and our past mistakes, knowing that mercy has already met us, that His compassion is not only present but abundant. Today, you are held in mercy, no matter where you've been or what you've walked through.

Let mercy find you today, wherever you are, in the midst of your struggles, your doubts, or your weariness. It's already waiting for you, ready to breathe life and hope into the moments that seem the hardest. Every time we receive God's mercy, we are reminded that no matter the darkness we face, His light and love will always lead us through. And it will be new, again and again, every single day.

Pause and Practice:
Take a deep breath, releasing any weight you carry. Whisper, Your mercies are new today. Let those words fill your spirit and settle deep in your heart, knowing that each breath you take is infused with God's unfailing love and mercy. Receive them fully, knowing that with each new day, His grace is sufficient, and His love never runs out.

Listen: "His Mercy Is More"

Week 3:
Abiding in Christ

Day 13 - Abide

Scripture: John 15:4 – *"Abide in me, and I in you. As the branch cannot bear fruit by itself, unless it abides in the vine, neither can you."*

Reflection:

To abide is more than just a passing moment, it is a lifestyle, a posture of intentional connection. Jesus doesn't merely ask us to visit Him or to check in occasionally. He invites us into a deep, transformative relationship that is sustained by constant, daily presence. To abide is to dwell in Him, to make our home in His love, and to remain anchored in His grace. It is a call to stay rooted in His truth, to allow His words to become our foundation, and to trust that in Him, we find our true identity and purpose.

When we abide, we are not simply checking off religious tasks or fulfilling obligations. We are invited into an ongoing relationship of intimacy and trust, where every moment of our day becomes an opportunity to stay close to Him. Abiding in Christ is not about achieving spiritual perfection; it's about the daily decision to stay connected, to lean into His presence, and to draw our strength, peace, and joy from Him. It is a choice to rely on His power rather than our own, to let His life flow into us and through us.

So often, we get caught up in striving. We push ourselves to do more, to be more, to prove our worth. We measure success by what we accomplish, not by the closeness of our connection to God. But Jesus offers us a different way. In His invitation to abide, He shows us that life in Him is not about effortful striving, it's about surrendering to the flow of grace, about trusting that our true identity and purpose come not from what we do, but from who we are in Him. It's about allowing His presence to fill us so completely that everything else flows naturally from there.

The branch does not worry about producing fruit, it simply stays attached to the vine. The vine is the source of life, the power that nourishes, sustains, and grows the branch. The branch's sole responsibility is to remain connected to the vine, to draw life from it, and to trust that in time, fruit will come. It doesn't rush, it doesn't strive, and it certainly doesn't force its growth. It simply abides.

In the same way, we are called to trust that God's work in us is not about us striving for perfection or forcing fruit to appear in our lives. It is about resting in His presence, letting His grace nourish and sustain us, and trusting that, in time, the fruit of the Spirit will naturally emerge. Love, joy, peace, patience, kindness, goodness, faithfulness, gentleness, and self-control will grow in us, not because we're striving to produce them, but because we are remaining in Him, abiding in His presence, and allowing His life to flow into ours.

This Lent, let go of the pressure to force growth or achieve spiritual success. Instead, focus on staying close to the Source. Every time you feel the weight of striving or self-doubt, remember that you don't need to fight for growth or success, just stay connected to the Vine. Abiding is not a passive act, but a deeply active one. It requires us to choose Him daily, to make space for Him in our hearts, and to trust that He is working in us, even when we can't see it right away.

When we abide in Christ, we are no longer driven by the need to perform, to impress, or to achieve. We are free to rest in the truth that we are already loved, already accepted, and already called. Our identity is secure in Him, and our fruit will come, not by our effort, but through His grace. The more we stay close to Jesus, the more we reflect His character and bear fruit that will last.

Abiding in Christ is not a task, but a relationship. It's about choosing to stay in His presence, day after day, trusting that in His timing, He will transform us. As we let go of our need for control and simply remain in Him, we discover the true peace that comes from knowing we are exactly where we need to be: in His arms, connected to the Vine, and living in the flow of His grace.

Pause and Practice:
Picture yourself as a branch held by the Vine. Whisper, Jesus, I choose to stay connected to You.

Listen: "Abide with Me"

Day 14 - Word

Scripture: Hebrews 4:12 – *"For the word of God is alive and active. Sharper than any double-edged sword..."*

Reflection:

Scripture is not just a collection of ancient texts or words printed on pages; it is the living breath of God, breathed out to us for transformation. The Word of God is alive, and its power is ongoing, constantly working to shape and mold us. It is not static or lifeless; it pulses with divine energy, ready to penetrate the deepest parts of our hearts and minds. Like a double-edged sword, the Word cuts through the confusion, exposing the deepest parts of our being. It doesn't just challenge our thoughts; it transforms our very lives.

In its sharpness, the Word brings clarity to the areas of our lives clouded by doubt and fear. It reveals truth where deception may have settled in and brings light to the dark corners of our hearts. Scripture doesn't just inform us intellectually; it convicts us and heals us in ways that are profound and lasting. The Word of God has the power to break down walls we've built around our hearts, to untangle the knots in our minds, and to restore the brokenness within us. It is a tool of both transformation and restoration, working in us and through us as we read it with open hearts.

During Lent, reading Scripture is not a task to check off a list or a ritual to complete, it is a feast for our souls. It is a meal meant to be savored, not rushed through. Just as our bodies need food for nourishment, our spirits need the Word of God to grow and be strengthened. This season of Lent invites us to draw nearer to the Scriptures, to allow them to dwell in us richly, to allow them to take root in our hearts and shape our thinking, living, and loving.

The Word of God isn't just something we turn to when we need answers; it is a wellspring of life that continually nourishes us. It offers us direction, wisdom, and understanding when we feel lost, weary, or uncertain. But more than that, it shapes us into the image of Christ, molding our character and our hearts into vessels of His grace.

As you immerse yourself in Scripture this Lent, let it be more than a mental exercise. Let it become a transformative experience. Allow the Word to cut through the clutter of your life, to convict, to heal, and to restore. Let it renew your mind and spirit. Let it lead you into deeper intimacy with God. Just as food sustains the body, the Word of God sustains the soul, filling us with wisdom, peace, and the power to live the life God has called us to.

This Lent, don't approach Scripture as a box to check but as an invitation to sit at the table with God, to feast on His Word, and to allow it to shape every part of who you are. Let it be alive in you, active and powerful, transforming the way you think, live, and love.

Pause and Practice:
Open your Bible. Read slowly. What word or phrase stands out? Meditate on it throughout the day.

Listen: "Ancient Words"

Day 15 - Presence

Scripture: Psalm 16:11 – *"You make known to me the path of life; in your presence there is fullness of joy."*

Reflection:

God's presence is not something confined to moments of religious rituals or spiritual mountaintops. It isn't limited to Sunday services, prayer retreats, or perfectly "spiritual" times. Rather, God's presence is pervasive and accessible right here, right now. Wherever you are, whether at work, with your family, in the quiet of your home, or even during your daily struggles, God is with you. The truth is, we often miss Him because we're looking for something extraordinary, hoping for a moment of overwhelming emotion or a spiritual high. We think we need to feel something specific to know He's near. But the reality is that His presence is not about a feeling; it's about a relationship.

The invitation of Psalm 16:11 is to recognize that God is always near, guiding us on the path of life and offering us the fullness of joy. But in order to experience that joy, we need to slow down and pay attention to the subtle ways He's at work in our lives. We need to become aware of the quiet whisper of His voice, the gentle nudge of His spirit, and the reminder of His love that is woven into the fabric of every moment. The practice of God's presence isn't about a heightened emotional experience; it's about learning to see, hear, and respond to Him in the everyday moments of life.

When we practice presence, we begin to notice God not just in the quiet times of prayer or worship, but in the busy, ordinary moments too. He's with us when we're stuck in traffic, when we're sitting down to a meal, when we're comforting a friend, or when we're going through challenges. Sometimes, we think joy will come when everything is perfect, when the problems of life disappear, when everything goes our way. But joy isn't the result of our circumstances being ideal; it's the result of knowing that God is with us in the middle of them. Joy doesn't always look like laughter or celebration; it often looks like peace in the middle of chaos, contentment during struggle, and hope even when we can't see the full picture.

The path of life that God makes known to us is not always straight or easy. It often winds through valleys, over rocky terrain, and through moments of confusion and difficulty. Yet, in each step, we are not walking alone. God's presence is there, offering us guidance, comfort, and hope. And with His presence comes the fullness of joy, the kind of joy that sustains us, carries us, and strengthens us even when things are hard.

This joy isn't a fleeting emotion that comes and goes with the ups and downs of life; it's a deep, abiding sense of peace that comes from knowing we are held by God's love. It's a joy that can coexist with sadness, uncertainty, and pain because it is rooted in the truth of who God is and the relationship we share with Him. The joy found in God's presence is not dependent on everything being right; it comes from knowing that no matter what, He is with us.

In the busyness of life, it's easy to forget that God's presence is always with us. We get distracted by our tasks, our worries, and the noise of the world. But joy comes when we take time to recognize His presence, to pause and reflect, to thank Him for His constant companionship. It's in those moments of stillness, when we acknowledge that He is here with us, that the fullness of joy begins to fill our hearts.

So, today, take time to practice God's presence. Slow down, breathe deeply, and recognize that He is with you right where you are. His joy is not a far-off promise; it's a present reality. Even in the mundane or the difficult, His presence offers you peace, guidance, and fullness of joy. Let go of the expectation that joy comes only when everything is perfect, and instead, embrace the truth that joy is found in the relationship, the relationship you have with the One who is always with you. His presence is a gift, and in it, there is always more joy to be found.

Pause and Practice:
Pause. Look around. Whisper, 'God, I know You're here.' Welcome His nearness today.

Listen: "Surely the Presence of the Lord Is in This Place"

Day 16 – Listen

Scripture: Isaiah 30:21 – *"Your ears shall hear a word behind you, saying, 'This is the way, walk in it.'"*

Reflection:

God is still speaking to us today. The question is not whether He is speaking, but whether we are listening. In the midst of life's noise and busyness, the voice of God can often feel distant or drowned out by the distractions around us. But His voice is still present, waiting for us to pause, tune in, and hear the whisper of the Spirit. It's in the stillness, in the sacred moments of reflection, and within the depths of our spirit where God often speaks most clearly. He speaks through Scripture, through the promptings of our heart, and through the quiet of our own thoughts when we choose to listen.

Listening to God requires more than just hearing the words; it demands a posture of attentiveness, responsiveness, and openness. In a world where our attention is pulled in a thousand directions, we must intentionally make space to hear God's voice. This requires slowing down, quieting our hearts, and becoming still before Him. It's easy to hear the noise of life; the conversations, the media, the constant hum of activity; but the voice of God calls to us in the quiet places. It is in those moments of stillness that we can hear the gentle, guiding word that says, "This is the way, walk in it."

Listening to God is an active choice. It's more than passive hearing; it's about opening our hearts and minds to His will and His direction. God does not force Himself upon us but lovingly invites us to follow His leading. When we listen, we invite God to guide us, to correct us, and to comfort us. Listening allows God to call us into a deeper relationship with Him, to reveal His plans for our lives, and to provide the wisdom we need for each step we take.

God's guidance doesn't always come in dramatic moments. Often, it comes as a quiet whisper, a subtle nudge, or a soft word that gently directs us on the right path. But this requires patience and trust. It means we must have the humility to pause and trust that God's way is better than our own. His voice may not always be loud, but it is always clear, and when we choose to listen, we can be confident that we are walking in the path He has set for us.

In moments of uncertainty or confusion, God promises to guide us. He is faithful to speak, even in the midst of our questions or doubts. But we must be willing to listen. Listening to God is not just about seeking answers; it's about learning to be in tune with His heart, trusting that He is always present and always willing to guide us when we are ready to listen.

Today, take time to listen. Be still and quiet your heart. Seek God's voice through prayer, reflection, and His Word. Trust that He is speaking and open yourself to hear His guidance. As you listen, allow Him to lead, correct, comfort, and call you. In doing so, you will walk the path of life with confidence, knowing that His voice is guiding you every step of the way.

Pause and Practice:
Ask, 'God, what are You saying to me today?' Then take two minutes to simply listen in stillness.

Listen: "Speak, O Lord"

Day 17 - Dwell

Scripture: Psalm 27:4 – *"One thing I ask... that I may dwell in the house of the Lord all the days of my life."*

Reflection:

David's one desire, expressed so powerfully in Psalm 27, was not for wealth, success, or even safety; it was to dwell in the house of the Lord all the days of his life. In the midst of the trials, the battles, and the pressures of life, David longed for nothing more than the continual presence of God. For him, being in God's presence was the highest goal and the deepest joy. This single desire shaped his life, priorities, and relationship with God. It wasn't about achieving anything in the world; it was about staying close to the heart of God.

Lent invites us into the same kind of desire. We are called to set aside the distractions and busyness of life, to pause and reflect on what truly matters. Like David, we are invited to long for the presence of God; not as something we visit occasionally, but as the place we choose to dwell. To dwell in God's presence means to make it our home, not a temporary resting place like a hotel. It's about cultivating a lifestyle of intimacy and awareness, where every part of our day, every activity, and every thought is lived in the reality of His nearness.

David's desire to dwell in the house of the Lord wasn't about a physical building, but about a constant, unbroken relationship with God. The "house of the Lord" represents more than just a location; it symbolizes a place of refuge, peace, and relationship. It is where God's presence dwells, where we find comfort, direction, and transformation. And just as David sought to dwell in that space, we too are called to carry His presence with us, to seek Him in the quiet moments, and to make room for Him in our hearts every day.

To dwell in the house of the Lord means to live with an awareness of His nearness. It's about inviting Him into the everyday rhythms of life; whether in our work, our rest, or our relationships. It's not just about a specific time or place where we meet with God; it's about cultivating a posture of the heart that keeps us open to His presence at all times. We can dwell with God in every moment, every circumstance, and every interaction.

In the busyness of our daily lives, it can be easy to forget that God is always near. But Lent offers us the opportunity to pause and intentionally focus on His presence. It's a time to reset our priorities, to create space for silence, and to open our hearts to deeper communion with Him. This season calls us to slow down and to intentionally dwell with God, not just as a temporary refuge, but as a permanent, sacred space where we live and breathe.

To dwell with God is an act of devotion. It's about choosing Him first, making time for Him in the midst of our responsibilities, and remembering that He is always with us. Whether we are working, serving, or resting, we can cultivate an awareness of His presence that transforms our daily lives into holy moments.

So today, make space to dwell with God. Set aside time to be in His presence, to pray, to reflect, and to listen. But also, invite Him into the moments that might seem mundane. Let your life become a constant place where His presence resides, and let His nearness shape how you think, live, and love. Make God your home, not just your destination, and let this desire to dwell in His presence be the one thing that guides your heart through each day.

Pause and Practice:
Find a quiet corner or simple moment to just be with God. Say, You are my dwelling place!

Listen: “Better Is One Day”

Day 18 - Rest

Scripture: Matthew 11:28 – *"Come to me, all you who are weary and burdened, and I will give you rest."*

Reflection:

Rest is not a luxury reserved for a few; it is a gift freely given to all who are willing to receive it. In the midst of a world that pushes us to constantly do more, achieve more, and hustle endlessly, Jesus offers an invitation to rest, to stop striving, and to simply be. His invitation is not just for those who are physically tired, but for all who are weary in heart and soul, burdened by the weight of expectations, responsibilities, and the constant pressure to perform. Jesus offers us rest that goes beyond mere relaxation; it is a deep, soul-level peace that only He can provide.

Rest in Christ is a powerful act of surrender. It is the release of all the things that weigh us down: the need to prove ourselves, the pressure to live up to the world's standards, and the exhausting pace we often set for ourselves. In His rest, we are invited to let go of the idea that our worth is tied to what we do. You are not defined by how much you accomplish, but by how deeply you are loved by God. Your identity is secure in Christ, and it is in Him that you find your truest sense of peace and belonging.

Lent offers us a unique opportunity to slow down and reflect on the rhythm of our lives. It's not just about doing less; it's about learning to rest more fully in Jesus. We are often so focused on doing, on achieving, and on meeting deadlines that we forget the importance of simply resting in His presence. True rest is not found in escaping the demands of life, but in embracing God's grace in the midst of them. Rest is about shifting our perspective; from striving to grace, from doing to being. It's a reminder that our ultimate peace is found not in external circumstances changing, but in the unshakable love and grace of Jesus.

When we come to Jesus, we come to the one who knows our burdens intimately. He is not distant or aloof; He is with us in our weariness. His heart is full of compassion for those who are tired and heavy-laden, and He calls us to bring our burdens to Him. In His presence, we find a rest that heals our hearts, a peace that passes understanding. It is the kind of rest that replenishes our strength, renews our spirit, and refocuses our hearts on what truly matters.

True rest in Christ invites us to live with a deeper sense of trust. It's about releasing our need to control every outcome and instead trusting that God is working all things together for our good. It's about laying down our worries, our anxieties, and our need for perfection and finding rest in the knowledge that God's grace is sufficient for us in every moment.

This Lent, take Jesus' invitation seriously. Don't simply try to do less; focus on resting more deeply in Him. Take time to pause, to be still, and to listen to His voice. Let go of the burdens that weigh you down and allow His love to fill you with peace. The rest He offers isn't just a temporary break; it's a deep, spiritual rest that restores your soul. It's an invitation to let His grace be enough, to trust that in Him, you can find the rest you need, not just for a moment, but for every day.

As you rest in Jesus, remember that His arms are always open to you. You don't have to prove yourself or earn His love. You are already deeply loved, and in His love, you find the rest you were created to enjoy.

Pause and Practice:
Name one burden you're carrying. Breathe deeply. Whisper, I receive Your rest today, Lord.

Listen: “Come Unto Me, Ye Weary”

Week 4:
Loving Like Jesus

Day 19 - Compassion

Scripture: Colossians 3:12 – *"Clothe yourselves with compassion, kindness, humility, gentleness and patience."*

Reflection:

Compassion begins with seeing; not just with our eyes, but with our hearts. Jesus' compassion was not a distant or abstract feeling; it was a deep, active response to the people around Him. He saw beyond the outward appearance and the surface-level interactions, and He looked into the heart of every person He encountered. He saw their pain, their struggles, their hopes, and their brokenness. To love like Jesus means learning to look deeper, to see beyond the flaws, the masks, and the walls people put up to protect themselves. It means being willing to let your heart break open for others, just as Jesus' heart broke for those He encountered.

Compassion isn't always about having the answers or fixing the problem. In our culture, we often associate love and compassion with "solving" issues, but Jesus shows us that sometimes, the most compassionate thing we can do is simply show up. Sometimes compassion looks like sitting quietly with someone in their pain, listening to their story without judgment, or just being present in their moment of need. It's not about trying to "fix" someone's situation; it's about showing them that they are seen, heard, and loved; just as they are.

In Colossians 3:12, we are called to clothe ourselves with compassion, kindness, humility, gentleness, and patience. These qualities are not just actions; they are postures of the heart. To clothe yourself with compassion is to put on a mindset that sees others with empathy, not judgment. It is choosing to respond with kindness, even when it's difficult, and with humility, knowing that we, too, need grace. Compassion requires gentleness and patience, for it is not about rushing in to fix things, but walking alongside others in a spirit of understanding and care.

When we ask God to soften our hearts, we are asking Him to help us see others the way He sees them, through eyes of grace, mercy, and love. This doesn't mean ignoring faults or pretending everything is perfect, but it does mean choosing to view others with a heart that is open and willing to offer the love and care they need. It's about recognizing that everyone is carrying something, and the simple act of acknowledging their pain can bring healing.

Today, ask God to open your eyes to see the people around you; not just in the way they present themselves, but in the way God sees them. Ask Him to soften your heart, to replace judgment with empathy, and to lead you into deeper acts of compassion. As you clothe yourself with compassion, kindness, humility, gentleness, and patience, you will begin to reflect the heart of Jesus more fully. Compassion becomes not just something we do, but who we become, an outpouring of God's love to a world in desperate need of His grace.

Pause and Practice:
Who needs your compassion today? Offer kindness freely—even in small, unnoticed ways.

Listen: "Let Your Heart Be Broken"

Day 20 - Serve

Scripture: Mark 10:45 – *"For even the Son of Man did not come to be served, but to serve..."*

Reflection:

Service is love in action. Jesus knelt to wash feet, fed the hungry, and healed the hurting. To follow Him is to serve; humbly, quietly, generously. No act of love is too small to matter.

We serve not to be noticed, but to reflect God's heart. Lent offers many opportunities to live for others. Serving changes the world, and it changes us.

Pause and Practice:
Do one small act of service today with no expectation of recognition or return.

Listen: "Make Me a Servant"

Day 21 - Wash

Scripture: John 13:14 – *"Now that I, your Lord and Teacher, have washed your feet, you also should wash one another's feet."*

Reflection:

Washing feet in Jesus' time was considered the lowliest, most menial task. It was reserved for servants, those with no status or recognition. Yet, in this intimate moment with His disciples, Jesus chose to perform this act of humble service, not to show His power or status, but to demonstrate the very essence of love. He, the Lord of all, bent low to wash the feet of those who would one day carry His message to the world. This act was not just about cleanliness; it was about modeling a life of humility, sacrifice, and selfless service.

To wash another's feet is to meet them in their mess, to embrace them in their brokenness, and to serve them without expectation of anything in return. It is to love without judgment, to offer care when it's not convenient, and to see the value of another person regardless of their status, appearance, or past. Jesus didn't wait for His disciples to clean themselves up before He served them. He washed their feet in all their imperfection, showing us that true love sees beyond the outward appearance and chooses to act with grace and kindness, no matter the circumstances.

While we may not be called to wash literal feet today, the spirit of Jesus' action remains the same. We are called to embrace an attitude of humility and service. Love often looks like the willingness to draw near to someone in their pain or struggle, to offer care in ways that may seem inconvenient or uncomfortable. It may look like choosing to listen when we're tired, offering help when it's not easy, or offering kindness to someone who is hard to love. Sometimes, love simply looks like picking up the towel and bowing our hearts low in service to others.

This kind of love requires intentional humility. It is not about seeking recognition or elevating ourselves through the act of serving. It is about coming alongside others with a heart of compassion and a willingness to serve without seeking personal gain. In a world that often values power, prestige, and status, Jesus' example is a radical call to embrace the lowly path, to wash the feet of others, and to offer love in the simplest, most humble ways.

As we reflect on this act of service, we are invited to look for opportunities to wash the feet of those around us; not literally, perhaps, but in the ways we care for them, love them, and meet their needs. In our relationships, in our communities, and even in our daily interactions, we are called to love with humility, to serve with grace, and to honor the humanity of others by meeting them in their mess, just as Jesus did for us.

Today, ask yourself: Where can I choose to serve with humility? Whose feet do I need to wash, not with water, but with my heart, my actions, and my time? True love often takes the form of a towel in hand and a heart that bows low. Let us embrace this calling with the same love and humility that Jesus demonstrated.

Pause and Practice:
Think of one humble, hands-on way you can serve someone today. Then do it with joy.

Listen: "The Basin and the Towel"

Day 22 - Kindness

Scripture: Ephesians 4:32 – *"Be kind and compassionate to one another, forgiving each other, just as in Christ God forgave you."*

Reflection:

Kindness, at its core, doesn't require agreement or shared perspectives; it simply requires love. In a world that is often quick to judge, slow to listen, and eager to criticize, kindness stands as a revolutionary act of grace. It is not about condoning wrongs or ignoring differences, but about offering love and compassion in the face of them. Kindness doesn't seek to win arguments or prove a point—it seeks to build bridges, soften hearts, and foster understanding. It opens doors where walls have been built, heals wounds where hurt has taken root, and ultimately reveals the heart of Jesus to a broken world.

In a culture that often rewards speed, efficiency, and the loudest voices, kindness is the quiet force that can make all the difference. We don't always know what others are carrying—the invisible burdens, the pain, the fears, or the struggles that they may be hiding behind a smile or a busy life. A kind word, a patient tone, a gentle touch—these seemingly small acts can be the light someone needs to make it through their day, or even their life. What may seem like a simple gesture to you might be the lifeline another person is desperately holding onto.

The beauty of kindness is that it transcends circumstance. It isn't dependent on how we feel or on how others treat us; it reflects God's love poured out through us. In Ephesians 4:32, we are called to be kind and compassionate, not because others necessarily deserve it, but because we, too, have been recipients of immeasurable kindness and grace through Christ. Our kindness is an echo of the love and forgiveness we've received from God, a reflection of His heart for humanity. Just as God forgave us in Christ, we are to forgive and show compassion to others, letting the same mercy that flows to us flow through us.

When we choose kindness, we become conduits of God's love and grace. It is through our kindness that people often see the face of Jesus. It may not always be in grand gestures, but in the everyday moments; when we listen patiently, when we speak gently, when we offer a hand of help without expecting anything in return. Let our kindness be an extension of Christ's love, not just in words, but in actions. Let it be the kind of kindness that touches lives, that disarms hostility, and that leads others to experience the transformative power of God's love.

Today, take a moment to reflect on how you can show kindness, not just to those who are easy to love, but also to those who challenge you. Choose to listen instead of judge, to forgive instead of hold grudges, to show compassion instead of indifference. You never know how your kindness may change the course of someone's day, or even their life. Let your kindness be an echo of Christ's love, a living testament to the grace you've received. In a world that desperately needs more love, let us be the ones who offer it.

Pause and Practice:
Be intentionally kind to someone today, even if they seem undeserving or difficult.

Listen: "They'll Know We Are Christians by Our Love"

Day 23 - Neighbor

Scripture: Luke 10:27 – *"Love your neighbor as yourself."*

Reflection:

When Jesus was asked, "Who is my neighbor?" He didn't respond with a simple definition or a list of criteria. Instead, He told a story—one that reveals the heart of what it means to love our neighbors. In the parable of the Good Samaritan (Luke 10:30-37), Jesus teaches that neighbor-love is not confined to those who are easy to love or those who look like us or think like us. Neighbor-love is about showing mercy to those in need, regardless of their background, race, or social status. It transcends boundaries of geography, politics, and personal comfort.

To love your neighbor as yourself means to go beyond yourself—to open your heart and mind to the needs of others. It requires noticing, caring, and acting on behalf of those around you. Loving your neighbor is not simply a passive feeling but an active choice. It's a call to see people not just as they appear on the outside, but as human beings worthy of dignity, care, and compassion. Jesus invites us to live beyond the limits of our own preferences, to move past our biases and prejudices, and to embrace a broader, more inclusive definition of love. Our neighbor is anyone we encounter, anyone who needs mercy, anyone whose life intersects with ours.

This kind of love is not always easy. In fact, sometimes your neighbor is the person who annoys you, the one who challenges your patience, or the one with whom you disagree. Loving those who rub us the wrong way or who make us uncomfortable requires supernatural grace. But in those moments, it's even more important to remember that love is not a feeling or a conditional response; it is a decision. When we love the unlovable, when we reach out to those who may not deserve our kindness or understanding, we reflect the heart of Jesus, who loved us when we were undeserving, when we were far from Him.

Sometimes your neighbor is the stranger, the outsider, the person society overlooks. It's the homeless person on the street, the single mother struggling to make ends meet, the elderly person living alone, or the refugee who's far from home. Loving them is not always convenient or comfortable. It might mean giving up your time, your resources, or your own sense of security. It might require you to step into someone else's pain, to walk alongside them in their brokenness, to sit with them in their suffering. But it is always holy. Jesus calls us to love not because it's easy or comfortable, but because it's a reflection of His love for us. He loved us sacrificially, even when it was costly, and we are called to do the same for those around us.

Loving our neighbors requires us to see them as Jesus sees them; worthy of love, worthy of mercy, and deserving of the care we would want for ourselves. When we love others as we love ourselves, we begin to see the world through the eyes of compassion, justice, and grace. We move from being passive bystanders to active participants in God's kingdom work on earth.

Today, take a moment to reflect on who your neighbors are. Consider not only those who are easy to love but also those who challenge you. Ask God to soften your heart and help you extend mercy to those who need it most. Neighbor love doesn't come naturally, but it is always holy, and a reflection of the love Christ has shown to us. Loving our neighbor as ourselves is a radical, transformative call that has the power to change lives, including our own. May this kind of love shape your interactions today and every day, and may it reflect the mercy and grace that God has so freely given you.

Pause and Practice:
Who have you overlooked? Reach out to someone today with love that crosses boundaries.

Listen: "Jesu, Jesu, Fill Us with Your Love"

Day 24 - Cross

Scripture: Galatians 6:14 – *"May I never boast except in the cross of our Lord Jesus Christ..."*

Reflection:

The cross is not just a symbol we wear around our necks or hang on a wall, it is the very foundation of our faith, a profound act of surrender and sacrifice. It is where the depth of God's love and the extent of His sacrifice converge, revealing a love that was willing to endure unimaginable pain and shame for the sake of humanity. Jesus did not go to the cross for His own benefit; He went there for us, out of a love so great that it chose death to bring us life. The cross is the ultimate demonstration of love, not in the form of sentimentality, but in the form of selflessness and complete surrender.

To love like Jesus is to take up our cross, not as a punishment, but as a purpose. The call to take up our cross is a call to self-sacrifice, to lay down our own desires, comforts, and even our own lives for the sake of others. This doesn't mean seeking suffering for the sake of suffering but rather choosing to follow Jesus' example of love in its most sacrificial form. The cross teaches us that love is not about convenience or self-preservation; it is about laying down what is comfortable, what is easy, and what is familiar for the sake of a greater purpose. The love that Jesus demonstrated on the cross wasn't about receiving something; it was about giving everything.

When Paul says, "May I never boast except in the cross," he is declaring that the only thing worthy of our pride, our attention, and our identity is the cross of Christ. In the cross, we find our salvation, our hope, and our identity as followers of Jesus. It is not in our achievements, our wealth, our popularity, or anything else that the world might boast in. The cross is the one place where we stand united, equal, and redeemed. It is the place where we are reminded that our worth is not found in our accomplishments but in the sacrifice of Christ on our behalf.

So, what are we willing to lay down for the sake of love? What parts of ourselves are we called to surrender to follow Jesus more faithfully? The cross is the ultimate lesson in selflessness, teaching us that genuine love comes at a cost. It requires us to lay down our pride, our comfort, our self-interest, and sometimes even our plans to embrace God's greater purposes. But in that cost, we discover the greatest gain: resurrection life. Through Jesus' death, we gain eternal life, freedom, and hope. His sacrifice becomes the gateway to new life, and we are invited to join in that resurrection story each day.

The cross is a paradox. It is a place of death, but it is also the place where life begins. In our surrender, we find freedom. In our loss, we find gain. In our death to self, we experience resurrection in Christ. When we choose to take up our cross, we are not just giving something up for the sake of sacrifice, but we are stepping into the fullness of life that Jesus offers. It is in the cross that we discover what it truly means to live; not for ourselves, but for the One who gave everything for us.

Today, reflect on what the cross means in your life. What is God calling you to lay down to follow Him more closely? What areas of your life are you holding onto that He is asking you to surrender? Remember that, just as the cross led to resurrection life for Jesus, it also leads to new life for us. As we surrender, we find the life God has always intended for us, full, abundant, and eternal. Let the cross be the center of your boast, the place where you find your identity, and the source of the love you offer to others.

Pause and Practice:
Reflect on what the cross means for you. What part of your life needs to surrender to love?

Listen: "When I Survey the Wondrous Cross"

Week 5:
Hope and Healing

Day 25 - Heal

Scripture: Jeremiah 30:17 – *"But I will restore you to health and heal your wounds,' declares the Lord."*

Reflection:

Healing is rarely a sudden, instantaneous event; it is a process, a journey that takes time, patience, and trust. It is not always a quick fix, but a deep and transformative work that God does within us. Whether we carry wounds in our bodies, our hearts, or our spirits, the promise of restoration remains constant. God declares that He will heal our wounds, not just the surface-level symptoms, but the very root of the pain. His healing touches the places we often try to hide, those areas of our lives that we have tucked away or tried to forget.

Our wounds can take many forms: physical pain, emotional scars from past trauma, relational hurts, or spiritual struggles that leave us feeling disconnected or lost. These wounds shape how we see the world and ourselves. They may be recent or long buried, but regardless of their origin, God promises to restore us. His healing doesn't just mask the pain or offer temporary relief; it is a restoration of our entire being. It is the deep, cleansing work that goes beyond what we can see or understand. The Healer, Jesus, touches every wound with compassion and care, offering us more than just comfort; He offers transformation.

When we invite God into our brokenness, we are not inviting Him to simply fix what is broken on the surface. We are asking Him to touch the deepest, most vulnerable parts of ourselves. Sometimes, the healing process is uncomfortable. It may evoke painful memories, deep-seated fears, or unresolved grief. But God is not afraid of our broken places. He does not turn away from our pain, nor does He condemn us for it. His presence is not distant or detached; He is near to those who are hurting. His heart is full of compassion, and His presence is what begins to heal us from the inside out.

Healing with God is not a passive experience. It requires us to open our hearts to Him, to be vulnerable with our pain, and to trust that His love is sufficient to restore us. The process may take time, but each step of the journey is marked by His presence. As we walk with God, we begin to experience His healing touch in profound ways, emotionally, physically, and spiritually. We learn to trust that He is working in us, even when we cannot see the full picture.

Whether your pain is fresh or long-buried, God is inviting you to invite Him in. No wound is too deep, no pain too great, for His healing touch. He is the Great Physician, and He can restore all things. His promise of healing extends not only to the body, but also to the heart and soul.

Today, pause and reflect on the areas of your life where healing is needed. Invite God into those places, no matter how painful or uncomfortable it may feel. Trust that He is not afraid of your brokenness. His love is the balm for your wounds, and His presence is the source of all healing. Let His healing begin to touch the deepest parts of your being, restoring you to wholeness and peace.

Pause and Practice:
Place your hand over your heart. Whisper, 'Lord, begin healing what I cannot fix on my own.'

Listen: "There Is a Balm in Gilead"

Day 26 - Restore

Scripture: Psalm 23:3 – *"He restores my soul. He leads me in paths of righteousness for his name's sake."*

Reflection:

Restoration is not merely a process of repair; it is the beautiful and complete renewal of what has been broken, worn down, or lost. When we think of restoration, we often picture something being patched up or fixed temporarily. But the restoration God offers is far greater; it's a transformation that brings us back to wholeness. He doesn't just put a bandage on our wounds or cover over our pain. He makes us new! God's restorative work in us is deep and complete, reaching into every area of our lives: our hearts, our minds, and our spirits.

Psalm 23 speaks to this profound restoration. "He restores my soul" is a declaration of God's faithful care, a reminder that our deepest needs, those hidden places of brokenness, despair, and weariness, are tended to by the Shepherd. Just as a shepherd lovingly cares for each sheep, gently guiding and protecting them, so too does God care for us. He leads us not just to a place of temporary relief, but to a place of true restoration, where we are made whole again in His presence.

Lent is an invitation to return to the Shepherd, the one who knows our needs even before we express them. It's a time to be reminded that restoration is not only possible but also promised by God. This journey of renewal may look different for each of us. For some, restoration may come in the form of rest, taking time to pause and reflect, allowing God to restore our physical and emotional energy. For others, it may come through repentance, as we turn away from the burdens we have carried and allow God to forgive and heal us. For some, it may mean receiving God's love again; letting His compassion and grace wash over us, filling the empty and weary places within.

Whatever form it takes, God's restoration is always gentle, patient, and complete. He doesn't rush the process; He tenderly and faithfully leads us, guiding us to paths of righteousness. These paths are not just about doing the right thing, but about finding the way that leads to healing, peace, and alignment with God's purpose for our lives. The Shepherd leads us beside still waters, restores our souls, and gently brings us back to wholeness, so that we can walk in His ways; not out of obligation, but for His name's sake, as a reflection of His goodness.

If you feel weary, burdened, or distant from God, this Lent is the perfect time to return to the Shepherd and allow Him to restore your soul. He is not a distant observer of your pain; He is the one who walks beside you, who heals, who renews. Let Him restore what weariness and worry have worn down in you. Allow His gentle guidance to lead you into a place of rest, renewal, and peace. When we return to the Shepherd, we find that He does not just restore what was lost; He makes us new, guiding us to the life He has always desired for us. Let God lead you in paths of righteousness and find the deep renewal that only He can provide.

Pause and Practice:
Pray: 'Good Shepherd, restore my soul today. Lead me gently back to life in You.'

Listen: "He Restoreth My Soul"

Day 27 - Peace

Scripture: John 14:27 – *"Peace I leave with you; my peace I give you. I do not give to you as the world gives..."*

Reflection:

Peace, as the world often defines it, is the absence of trouble or conflict. It's found in moments of quiet, in spaces where everything is calm and under control. However, the peace that Jesus offers is something entirely different. His peace is not a fleeting moment of relief from chaos; it is the presence of Christ Himself. It is not dependent on circumstances, external stability, or the absence of pain. The peace Jesus gives transcends the storms of life, it is deep and unshakable because it flows from knowing who holds your heart.

When Jesus tells His disciples, "My peace I give you," He offers something far beyond the temporary sense of calm the world provides. The peace He provides is not circumstantial; it does not come and go based on the ebb and flow of life. It is a peace that remains amidst confusion, anxiety, and hardship. It is rooted in the unchanging reality of God's presence with us. Jesus' peace doesn't promise a life free from trials; instead, it promises His presence during them. The world's peace is based on the hope that everything will align perfectly and be comfortable, but the peace that Christ offers remains even when things don't go as planned.

To embrace the peace that Jesus gives is to let go of the counterfeit peace we often seek. So often, we look for peace in places that are temporary and uncertain, control, comfort, and certainty. We try to manage situations and people in ways that will give us a sense of security, only to find that the moment we feel like we've got everything under control, something shifts, and our peace is lost.

This kind of peace is fragile and unreliable, easily disrupted by the unpredictable nature of life.

Instead, Jesus calls us to let go of this shallow, conditional peace and to embrace the deep, unshakable peace that comes from trusting God in the midst of the storm. True peace is not the absence of difficulty, but the presence of Christ amid it. It is the peace that says, "Even though I don't understand what is happening around me, I trust that God is with me. Even though I feel anxious or uncertain, I know that He is in control." This peace is built on a firm foundation of trust in God's love, faithfulness, and sovereignty, regardless of what the world may throw at us.

This peace allows us to walk through life with calm assurance, knowing that we are never alone. It gives us the strength to face life's challenges without being shaken, the courage to step into the unknown with confidence, and the patience to endure through difficulties. It is a peace that isn't temporary, a peace that doesn't rely on the world's standards of success, comfort, or control. It is a peace that passes all understanding, one that guards our hearts and minds in Christ Jesus.

Today, reflect on the peace that Jesus offers you. Let go of the false peace that comes from trying to control everything and embrace the deep, lasting peace that only He can provide. Trust Him to hold your heart during the storm, and let His peace guard you, guide you, and sustain you. When we place our trust in God's presence and His sovereignty, we discover that His peace is more than enough, unchanging, unwavering, and always available.

Pause and Practice:
Take three slow breaths. With each whisper: 'Jesus, fill me with Your peace.'

Listen: "It Is Well with My Soul"

Day 28 - Joy

Scripture: Nehemiah 8:10 – *"Do not grieve, for the joy of the Lord is your strength."*

Reflection:

Joy and grief can coexist. While they may seem like opposites, they are not mutually exclusive. In fact, it is often in the midst of our sorrow that the deepest joy is found. Lent creates space for both, allowing us to bring our grief, our pain, and our loss before God, while also inviting His joy to heal and strengthen us. The joy of the Lord is not a superficial happiness that ignores the reality of our struggles. It is a profound, soul-deep joy that transcends circumstances and stands firm even in the face of difficulty.

Joy doesn't always come in loud, jubilant moments. Sometimes, it's a quiet, steady assurance that God is good, even in the hardest of times. This kind of joy doesn't minimize our pain; it meets us in it. It doesn't dismiss the weight of grief or the depth of loss, but it stands alongside it, acknowledging it, and gently singing a song of hope. The joy of the Lord is not a denial of our suffering; it is a comfort amid it, a reminder that we are not alone, and that God's presence with us is a source of unshakable hope.

You were made for joy. It's a part of who you are, deeply rooted in your very being as a child of God. It's not a fleeting emotion but a deep, lasting gladness that comes from knowing you are loved, cherished, and held by the Creator of the universe. This joy is a strength that can sustain us when everything else feels fragile. It doesn't come from our circumstances, our achievements, or our own efforts. It comes from God, from knowing that He is with us and that His love is unchanging. His joy is a strength that is born not from fear, but from a deep trust in His goodness.

Amid your grief, your weariness, or your struggle, let God's love stir joy in your soul today. Let it be a quiet, steady flame that burns even when life is difficult. This joy is a wellspring of strength that enables us to persevere, to endure, and to find hope, even when the road is hard. The joy of the Lord doesn't promise an absence of pain, but it promises a presence that transforms pain into purpose, grief into grace, and weakness into strength.

As you walk through this season, remember that joy is not the absence of sorrow; it is the presence of God's love and strength during it. Allow His joy to be your strength today, no matter what you are facing. You were made for joy, and in God's presence, that joy can be the strength that carries you through every trial, every storm, and every season of grief.

Pause and Practice:
Smile today, for no reason but grace. Let your joy be an offering of thanks.

Listen: "Joyful, Joyful, We Adore Thee"

Day 29 - Wait

Scripture: Isaiah 40:31 – *"But those who wait on the Lord shall renew their strength..."*

Reflection:

Waiting often feels like doing nothing. In a world that values productivity and instant results, waiting can feel like wasted time, a frustrating pause in the journey. But in God's kingdom, waiting is not only powerful; it is transformative. Waiting is not passive; it is an active, intentional surrender to God's timing and plan. It is in the waiting that God often works most deeply in us, shaping our character, refining our hearts, and strengthening our trust in Him.

Waiting stretches our faith. It challenges us to trust when we can't see the way forward, when the answers aren't clear, and when the promise seems far off. But in this stretching, our dependence on God deepens. We are reminded that we cannot control everything, that we are not the ones who bring about the results. It is God's timing, His sovereignty, and His faithfulness that carry us through the waiting seasons of life. Though we may not see the fruit immediately, God is working behind the scenes, preparing us and preparing the promise.

The process of waiting is often uncomfortable. It requires patience, trust, and surrender. But waiting is holy. It is in these moments that we are drawn closer to God, learning to rely on His provision, His timing, and His guidance. The strength we receive in the waiting comes from the Lord, and it is this strength that sustains us through the next phase of the journey. Those who wait on the Lord shall renew their strength; strength not of our own making, but strength that flows from His presence.

In the season of waiting, we may feel like we are stagnant or stuck. But God is not idle; He is at work in ways we cannot always see. He is preparing us, molding us, and aligning our hearts with His will. He is also preparing the promise, ensuring that everything is in place for His perfect timing. The waiting period is never wasted in God's hands; it is a season of growth, preparation, and deepening trust.

Don't rush this season. Let the waiting be holy. Recognize that God is at work even when you cannot see immediate results. Trust that He is preparing you for what is to come, and that His timing is always perfect. God is not late, He is preparing both you and the promise. As you wait, lean into His presence, rest in His faithfulness, and allow Him to renew your strength. The waiting will lead to something greater than you could imagine, and in the end, you will find that the strength you gained in the waiting has equipped you for what lies ahead.

Pause and Practice:
Sit for one minute in silence. Inhale, 'I wait.' Exhale, 'on You, Lord.'

Listen: "Teach Me, O Lord, to Wait"

Day 30 - Believe

Scripture: Mark 9:23 – *"Everything is possible for one who believes."*

Reflection:

Belief is often misunderstood as certainty, as knowing exactly how things will unfold, but in reality, belief is not about having all the answers or being sure of the outcome. It's about trust—choosing to believe that, even when the road ahead is unclear, the One who holds our future is good and faithful. To believe is to place our confidence not in the circumstances or the outcome, but in the character of God. It's saying, "I don't have to know how this ends to know Who holds it." Belief is not about controlling the details, but about trusting in the One who has already ordained them.

Belief is the seed of miracles, the spark that keeps hope alive even in the darkest moments. It is the quiet, persistent faith that whispers, "It's possible, even when it seems impossible." It's the trust that, despite the uncertainty, God is at work and will bring about His good purposes in His perfect timing. Even when everything around us feels uncertain, belief in God's goodness is what anchors us and keeps our hope alive.

In the passage from Mark, Jesus is speaking to a father whose son has been plagued with a debilitating condition for years. The father cries out to Jesus, "If you can do anything, take pity on us and help us." Jesus responds with the powerful statement, "Everything is possible for one who believes." This isn't a call to believe in outcomes or results; it is an invitation to believe in God's ability to do the impossible, to trust in His power, and to surrender our fears and limitations to Him.

Belief is not about having certainty in the outcome, but about having trust in the goodness of God, even when the situation seems dire. It's about knowing that God's plans are always for our good, even when we can't see how things will work out. Belief is the foundation of our faith, the bedrock that keeps us steady when fear threatens to overwhelm us. It's the first step toward seeing the miraculous unfold in our lives.

Ask God to strengthen your belief, not in the outcomes or the "how" of situations, but in His goodness. Faith is not the absence of fear, but the willingness to name our fear and surrender it to God. Faith begins where fear is acknowledged and surrendered to God, trusting that He is greater than our fears, more capable than we could ever imagine, and bigger than our doubts.

Today, take a step of belief, even in the midst of uncertainty. Trust that everything is possible for the one who believes, not because we know how things will unfold, but because we know the One who holds our future. Let your belief become the spark that ignites your hope, even when the road is unclear, and watch as God works miracles in your life, just as He has done throughout history.

Pause and Practice:
Pray: 'I believe, Lord. Help my unbelief.' Let that be enough today.

Listen: "Only Believe"

Week 6:
The Way of the Cross

Day 31 – The Way

Scripture: John 14:6 – *"I am the way and the truth and the life. No one comes to the Father except through me."*

Reflection:

In this powerful declaration, Jesus doesn't merely point us toward a path; He is the path. He is the Way, the Truth, and the Life. He is not just a guide who shows us how to reach God; He is the very means by which we have access to God. In His life, death, and resurrection, He makes a way where there was none. The road to the cross was not an accident or an afterthought; it was filled with pain and purpose. Every step Jesus took was one of intentionality, knowing that His sacrifice was the only way to reconcile humanity to God.

As we approach Holy Week, we are invited to walk the way of surrender, sacrifice, and salvation. The journey to the cross is not an easy one. It is a path of deep selflessness, a way that leads through suffering and death. Yet, it is also the road to resurrection and new life. To follow Jesus is to walk in His footsteps, to take up the cross of love, to endure trials with unwavering faith, and to remain hopeful in the face of despair. The path of Christ is not wide and easy; it is narrow, filled with obstacles and challenges. However, it is the only way that leads to true life, life in its fullest and most abundant form.

To walk the way of Jesus is to live a life of love that lays down its rights, its comforts, and its desires for the sake of others. Jesus demonstrated this love through His sacrifice on the cross, and He calls us to follow Him in the same way. It is a love that isn't about self-preservation but about self-giving. It is a love that loves even when it costs us, even when it's difficult, and even when it's painful. This is the love that brings healing and reconciliation.

To follow Jesus is also to walk in faith that endures. The way of the cross is not about avoiding suffering but about trusting in God's plan even when we cannot see the outcome. It's about having the faith to take each step, knowing that God's promises are true and that His presence is with us every step of the way. Faith in Jesus is a faith that holds firm through the storms of life, that trusts in His goodness even when we can't understand the suffering we endure.

Finally, to follow Jesus is to have hope that overcomes. The hope that Jesus offers is not a wishful thinking that ignores the reality of suffering; it is a hope that is grounded in the certainty of God's victory over sin and death. The way of the cross is a way of hope because we know that Jesus has already overcome the greatest enemy, death itself. His resurrection is the guarantee that our hope will never be in vain.

The way of Jesus is narrow, and it leads to life. It is a path of sacrifice, endurance, and overcoming. But it is also the only way that leads to true joy, peace, and fulfillment. As we enter Holy Week, we are invited to walk with Him on the road to the cross. In doing so, we are reminded that the way of surrender and sacrifice is not just the way to death, it is the way to life, and life abundantly.

Today, reflect on what it means to follow Jesus. What does it look like for you to walk His path of love, faith, and hope in your own life? Embrace the narrow way, knowing that it leads to eternal life with Him.

Pause and Practice:
Visualize yourself walking with Jesus. Whisper, 'Lead me on the way of the cross.'

Listen: "I Have Decided to Follow Jesus"

Day 32 - Betrayed

Scripture: Luke 22:48 – "Judas, are you betraying the Son of Man with a kiss?"

Reflection:

Betrayal cuts deep, and the pain of being betrayed is often hardest to bear when it comes from those closest to us. It is one thing to be hurt by a stranger, but when the wound comes from a friend, a confidant, or someone we trusted, it feels like a deeper, more personal betrayal. Jesus understood this pain all too well. He was not betrayed by an enemy, but by one of His own disciples, a man He had walked with, taught, and loved. Judas, with a kiss, an act meant to signify love and affection, sealed the betrayal that would lead to Jesus' arrest and crucifixion. The sting of betrayal in this moment is sharp and personal, yet Jesus' response is filled with grace, mercy, and even sorrow for Judas' actions. Despite being betrayed, He did not respond with hatred or vengeance but with love and understanding.

Jesus' ability to respond to betrayal with such grace is a testament to His divine nature and His ability to love even those who wrong Him. His question to Judas, "Are you betraying the Son of Man with a kiss?" reveals not just the depth of His pain but also His willingness to confront the betrayal with an open heart. In the midst of betrayal, Jesus did not turn away in bitterness. Instead, He stood in the face of injustice with a heart of love that called out the truth, offering Judas an opportunity to turn back.

Have you felt the sting of betrayal in your own life? Whether from a friend, a family member, a partner, or even someone in the church, the pain of being betrayed can leave lasting scars. The wounds can cause us to question our trust in others, to retreat into ourselves, or to harbor anger and bitterness. It's a natural human response to hurt in this way, but Jesus offers us another way. He invites us to bring our pain to Him, the One who understands betrayal better than anyone. He, who was betrayed by a close friend, has walked the path of hurt and rejection and now stands ready to heal and restore us.

On the other hand, maybe you've been the one who has betrayed someone else. The weight of guilt and regret can be just as heavy, and the fear of seeking forgiveness can prevent us from turning back. But just as Jesus extended grace to Judas, He offers that same grace to us. No matter how great the wrong, no matter how deeply we've hurt another, Jesus stands ready to forgive us completely. Lent is a time to reflect on both our wounds and our wrongs. It invites us to bring our betrayal, whether experienced or committed, to the One who forgives fully, knowing that in Him, we can find healing and restoration.

This season of Lent calls us to examine both the betrayals we have suffered and the times we have failed to honor those who trusted us. We are invited to take both our wounds and our wrongs to Jesus, the One who knows betrayal intimately but offers forgiveness and redemption fully. In His grace, we find the freedom to let go of anger and guilt, to release our pain, and to restore what has been broken. As we bring our hearts before Him, we can rest in the assurance that His love and forgiveness are greater than any hurt or wrong we have experienced or caused.

Today, reflect on the pain of betrayal in your life. Have you been betrayed? Have you betrayed someone? Bring these wounds before Jesus, knowing that He is ready to heal, to forgive, and to restore. Let the grace He offers transform the broken places in your heart, leading you toward reconciliation, peace, and healing.

Pause and Practice:
Bring a name to God; someone who hurt you, or someone you've hurt. Ask for grace to forgive or seek forgiveness.

Listen: "Go to Dark Gethsemane"

Day 33 - Denied

Scripture: Luke 22:61–62 – *"The Lord turned and looked straight at Peter... And he went outside and wept bitterly."*

Reflection:

Denial often arises from fear. Peter, a man who loved Jesus deeply, found himself in a moment of crisis where fear overtook his faith. Despite his earlier promises to stand by Jesus no matter what, fear of the consequences led him to deny knowing the very One he had followed and served. In the high-pressure moment, Peter's fear of being associated with Jesus in His darkest hour led to three denials. Yet, it was not anger or condemnation that Jesus turned toward Peter with; it was a look of deep compassion, understanding the root of Peter's fear and failure.

Peter's denial didn't take Jesus by surprise, but it did cause deep sorrow. The look that Jesus gave Peter in the courtyard was not one of judgment, but one filled with love and sorrow. It was a look that said, "I know you, and I know your heart. I see your struggle, and I see your pain." Jesus didn't abandon Peter in his darkest moment. Instead, He met Peter's eyes with grace and compassion, offering him a quiet invitation to repentance and restoration. That moment, painful as it was for Peter, also marked the beginning of his healing and redemption. Though Peter felt the weight of his failure, Jesus did not reject him.

Have you ever denied Christ in your own life? Maybe not with words, but through silence, shame, or compromise. Perhaps there have been times when fear, pride, or self-preservation led you to remain quiet when you should have spoken, to compromise when you should have stood firm, or to hide your faith when it felt unsafe. In those moments, it can feel as if we have distanced ourselves from God. But just as Jesus didn't abandon Peter, He does not abandon us in our failures. When we falter, He is still there, meeting us with love, not condemnation.

Jesus' look toward Peter was a reminder that, even in our weakest moments, His grace is greater than our failure. There is still room for repentance, restoration, and reconciliation. If you've denied Christ, whether in small ways or large, there is still grace. Jesus' love for you is unwavering, and He is ready to meet your eyes with that same compassion. His gaze does not condemn you; it invites you to return to Him, to acknowledge your shortcomings, and to experience the forgiveness He offers.

Lent is a time of reflection, repentance, and renewal. If there are areas in your life where you have denied Christ, through silence, fear, or compromise, bring those moments before Him today. Know that Jesus is not standing ready to condemn you, but to heal you. His love, even in the face of our denial, is constant and overflowing. As you bring your heart before Him, let His gaze be one of compassion and healing, and allow His grace to restore what has been broken. Just as Peter was restored after his failure, you too are invited to experience the full extent of God's love and mercy.

Pause and Practice:
Ask: Where have I distanced myself from Jesus? Let His look of mercy restore you.

Listen: "Jesus Is Tenderly Calling You Home"

Day 34 - Mocked

Scripture: Mark 15:17–18 – *"They put a purple robe on him, then twisted together a crown of thorns... And they began to call out to him, 'Hail, king of the Jews!'"*

Reflection:

In this moment, Jesus, the King of Glory, was mocked, humiliated, and scorned. The very One who held all power and authority was dressed in a purple robe, a symbol of royalty, but not in the way He deserved. The soldiers twisted a crown of thorns and forced it onto His head, an act that not only caused immense physical pain but also was an attempt to ridicule His claim to be King. As they mocked Him, calling out, "Hail, king of the Jews," they misunderstood the true nature of His kingship. They saw Him as weak and powerless, but in reality, He was bearing the weight of the world's sin and shame, enduring it for the salvation of humanity.

Jesus didn't endure this mockery and suffering for show; He bore it for a purpose. He willingly accepted the pain, the humiliation, and the rejection because He knew that His sacrifice would bring about the redemption of the world. The crown of thorns that pierced His brow was not a symbol of failure; it was a symbol of victory, the victory over sin, death, and every power that sought to separate us from God. Jesus' suffering on the cross was not meaningless; it was sacred. Every lash, every mockery, every thorn, and every moment of scorn had a purpose: to bring healing, forgiveness, and freedom to those who would believe in Him.

When you face mockery, misunderstanding, or rejection for your faith, remember that Jesus has already been there. He understands what it feels like to be misunderstood, to be scorned for His identity and His mission. He was mocked and ridiculed, yet

He remained steadfast in His love for us. His pain was not in vain; it has eternal significance. It means that no matter what suffering you may endure, Jesus has already gone before you, and He has made a way through the pain.

His suffering gives your pain sacred meaning. When you face difficulties, whether it's the rejection of others, the pain of loss, or the loneliness of standing for what you believe, you are not alone. Jesus bore the scorn so that you wouldn't bear your shame alone. He took on the worst of humanity's rejection so that you could find acceptance in God's love. His pain is your comfort. His suffering is your hope. In every moment of your struggle, you can know that He has walked that path before you, and He is with you now.

Lent invites us to reflect on this powerful act of love and sacrifice. As we meditate on Jesus' suffering, let us remember that His pain was for our salvation, and His crown of thorns was the beginning of His eternal reign as King. Let His suffering give you courage, strength, and hope, knowing that in Christ, our pain and suffering are never in vain. They are redeemed and made holy through His sacrifice.

Pause and Practice:
Bring your hurt and misunderstanding to the cross. Jesus knows. And He honors your endurance.

Listen: "O Sacred Head Now Wounded"

Day 35 - Carried

Scripture: John 19:17 – *"Carrying his own cross, he went out to the place of the Skull..."*

Reflection:

Jesus carried His own cross, a symbol of both the immense physical and emotional weight He was about to bear. Yet, He didn't carry it for His own guilt; He carried it for ours. Every step He took on that road was not for Himself, but for the redemption of humanity. He walked the road of suffering, not because He deserved it, but because He chose to endure it for our sake, offering us the possibility of freedom from sin and death. The cross, which would become a symbol of shame and pain, was also the pathway to salvation; a journey that would lead Jesus to the ultimate act of love.

Each step that Jesus took toward Golgotha, the "place of the Skull," was marked by an unparalleled love, a love so deep and sacrificial that it could not be measured by human standards. He did not resist the journey; He embraced it, knowing that in the suffering He would endure, He was making a way for us to be reconciled to God. Every step He took was one of obedience to the Father, one of mercy and grace for the lost, the broken, and the hurting. Jesus' willingness to carry the cross was a profound declaration of His love for us, that He would bear the weight of all our sin, our shame, and our guilt so that we could experience the freedom of forgiveness.

There are moments in life when our burdens feel too heavy to carry. The weight of grief, disappointment, anxiety, or fear can overwhelm us, and the road ahead can feel impossible. But Lent serves as a reminder that you do not carry your burden alone. Jesus, who carried the weight of the world's sin on His shoulders, is right there beside you, offering His strength. He knows what it feels like to carry a heavy load, and He is more than willing to help carry yours.

Christ has already borne the greatest weight, the weight of sin, and He invites us to bring our burdens to Him. He offers us not just His sympathy, but His active help, His sustaining presence, and His healing power. The cross Jesus carried was not just a symbol of His suffering; it was the symbol of His victory. In carrying our burdens, He has already triumphed over the forces that seek to break us. No matter how heavy the load, Jesus is here, walking with us, and offering to share in the weight we carry.

As we reflect on Jesus' journey to the cross, let us remember that He understands our pain, our struggles, and our burdens. He carried the weight of our sin, but He also promises to help carry our burdens, to give us rest, and to strengthen us along the way. Let each step of His journey remind us that we are never alone in our suffering; He is with us, bearing the weight of our pain, and offering the freedom that only His love can bring.

Pause and Practice:
Imagine Jesus beside you, helping you carry your cross. Whisper, Thank You for walking with me.

Listen: "Must Jesus Bear the Cross Alone?"

Day 36 - Forsaken

Scripture: Psalm 22:1 – *"My God, my God, why have you forsaken me? Why are you so far from saving me, so far from my cries of anguish?"*

Reflection:

In the midst of His deepest agony, as Jesus hung on the cross, He cried out in desperation: "My God, my God, why have you forsaken me?" These words, filled with sorrow and pain, are among the most profound and heartbreaking in Scripture. Jesus, the Son of God, felt the weight of complete abandonment; not just by His friends, but even by His Father. This moment of intense isolation was not a mere expression of despair; it was a deep spiritual reality that Jesus experienced as He bore the full weight of humanity's sin. For the first time in eternity, the perfect communion between Father and Son was broken as Jesus took upon Himself the sin of the world.

Jesus' cry of forsakenness reveals the depth of His suffering; not only physical, but emotional and spiritual. He entered the darkest place so that you would never have to be alone in yours. In that moment, He felt the crushing loneliness and separation that comes from sin, but He endured it for our sake. The silence of God on the cross was not an absence; it was a profound act of sacrifice. God, in His infinite love, allowed His Son to experience the full depth of human suffering so that we could be brought back into relationship with Him.

If you have ever felt forgotten, abandoned, or forsaken, whether by people, by circumstances, or by God, know that Jesus understands that pain. He experienced it in its fullest form. He knows the depths of human despair and isolation. His cry on the cross was not a moment of weakness; it was a powerful expression of His willingness to endure the full extent of our brokenness. Jesus' suffering was not in vain; it was for our redemption. He entered the silence of abandonment so that when we face our own moments of silence, we are not truly alone.

In the moments when you feel forgotten, remember that Jesus is with you in the silence. He does not abandon you in your pain or suffering. He meets you there, in the quiet and the darkness, with the same love that led Him to the cross. His silence on the cross was the ultimate sacrifice, and it is in this sacrifice that we find our hope.

Though Jesus cried out in forsakenness, His cry was not without purpose. His death on the cross was not the end of the story; resurrection was already on the horizon. In the silence of His death, new life was being birthed. The very moment that seemed like defeat was the moment that ushered in victory for all who would believe. No matter how dark the moment may seem, no matter how distant God may feel, remember that resurrection is already on the horizon. Just as Jesus rose from the dead, so too will He bring life into our darkest places, offering us hope, renewal, and the assurance that we will never face abandonment again.

Pause and Practice:
If you feel forsaken, say it honestly. Then say, Yet I trust You, Lord.

Listen: "Stricken, Smitten, and Afflicted"

Week 7:
Holy Week

Day 37 - Surrender

Scripture: Matthew 26:39 – *"My Father, if it is possible, may this cup be taken from me. Yet not as I will, but as you will."*

Reflection:

In the garden of Gethsemane, Jesus shows us the depth of surrender, not in moments of peace or certainty, but in the grip of agony and fear. As He faced the unimaginable suffering that lay ahead, He prayed not only with His heart but with His whole being; vulnerable, honest, and full of anguish. Jesus, in His humanity, asked God to take the cup of suffering away from Him, showing us that it's okay to express our fears, doubts, and desires before God. Yet, even in His distress, He did not shy away from the ultimate act of surrender: "Not as I will, but as you will."

Jesus didn't rush past His pain or try to ignore it. Instead, He wrestled with it in prayer, bringing His full self, His fear, His sorrow, His sense of abandonment, to His Father. His struggle in Gethsemane was not a rejection of God's will, but a faithful confrontation with it. In the garden, we see Jesus as both fully divine and fully human: the Savior who knew the Father's plan, yet the Son who felt the weight of it and wrestled with what that would mean for Him. Gethsemane teaches us that surrender is not a one-time event, but a process; one that may include fear, pain, and tears, but also faith, trust, and hope.

Lent leads us to this quiet garden, where Jesus, in His deepest moment of turmoil, showed us how to bring our full selves before God. We don't have to hide our questions, our struggles, or our moments of uncertainty. Jesus' prayer reveals that it's okay to be honest with God about our fears and our desires. Faith is not found in having all the answers or in being free from doubt.

Instead, faith is found in trusting God's heart, even in the dark, even when we don't understand His will.

Gethsemane teaches us that surrender isn't just about accepting the outcome; it's about trusting God in the process. Jesus' example shows us that surrender can be messy. It can involve wrestling with God, crying out in pain, and questioning what lies ahead. But the beauty of surrender is that it opens the door to peace; not because we have everything figured out, but because we have trusted God with our whole hearts. In that surrender, we find a deeper connection to God, a deeper trust in His will, and a deeper sense of His presence in our suffering.

As you reflect on Gethsemane, ask yourself: What are the areas of your life where you need to surrender to God's will? Are you willing to bring your full self, your fears, your tears, your questions, before Him in prayer? Remember, faith is not about having all the answers, but about trusting God's heart even when the path is unclear. Jesus shows us that surrender in the face of agony is not weakness, but strength; strength found in the peace that comes from trusting God, even in the darkest moments.

Pause and Practice:
Kneel or sit quietly. Whisper Jesus' prayer: Not my will, but Yours be done.

Listen: "Tis Midnight, and on Olive's Brow"

Day 38 – Crucified

Scripture: Luke 23:33 – *"When they came to the place called the Skull, they crucified him there..."*

Reflection:
The cross is where love was lifted high, where heaven and earth intersected in a way that could never be fully understood but would forever change the course of history. Jesus didn't die as a victim, passively enduring the cruelty of humanity. He chose to lay down His life in full authority and love. Every step He took toward the cross, every nail that pierced His hands and feet, every breath He drew in agony, was an act of complete submission to the Father's will. He willingly endured the cross, not because He was powerless, but because He was powerful enough to embrace the fullness of suffering for the sake of our salvation.

Jesus' suffering was not meaningless. It was for your healing, physically, emotionally, and spiritually. The wounds He bore on the cross were not simply marks of torture; they were marks of love, marks of a Savior who was willing to take on the weight of every sin, every hurt, every brokenness of the world. His body was broken, so that our brokenness could be healed. His pain became the pathway to our peace. As Isaiah 53:5 says, "By His wounds, we are healed." The cross was not just a symbol of death; it was the means of life, the place where redemption was secured for all who would believe.

Good Friday invites us to stand at the foot of the cross, not just in sorrow, but in awe. We are called to gaze upon the sacrifice made for us and to reflect on the profound mystery of God's love poured out in such a brutal way. In the midst of our sorrow, there is awe because we recognize the magnitude of what was done for us. This is not just a historical event; it is a personal act of love that affects our lives today. Jesus' willingness to suffer and die reflects His unwavering commitment to us, a commitment to offer forgiveness, grace, and eternal life.

At the foot of the cross, we see love in its purest and most sacrificial form. This is love; wounded, poured out, victorious. The cross reveals love that chooses the hard path, love that endures pain, love that overcomes every obstacle to bring salvation to the world. It is a love that does not retreat in the face of suffering, but embraces it fully for the sake of others. It is a love that conquers sin and death, and in doing so, invites us into the eternal peace that only Christ can offer.

On Good Friday, we are called to remember the depth of Jesus' sacrifice. We are invited to sit in the solemnity of His suffering, but also to stand in awe of His victory. The cross was not the end; it was the beginning of the greatest victory ever won. In the shadow of the cross, we find both sorrow and joy. Sorrow for the pain that was endured, but joy in the assurance that His sacrifice was enough to secure our salvation. This is the paradox of the cross, the greatest tragedy and the greatest triumph, both held together in love.

As you reflect on the cross, allow yourself to stand in awe of the depth of God's love for you. Jesus bore the weight of the cross, not for His own sake, but for yours. His suffering was for your healing, His wounds became your peace, and His death secured your life. Let this truth move you to worship, to gratitude, and to a deeper commitment to the One who laid down His life for you.

Pause and Practice:
Spend time in silence. Reflect on the cross. Pray, Thank You for the cross, Jesus. I will never forget.

Listen: "Were You There When They Crucified My Lord?"

Day 39 - Buried

Scripture: Matthew 27:59–60 – *"Joseph took the body... and placed it in his own new tomb."*

Reflection:

Between the cross and the resurrection, there is silence. After the intense suffering and the earth-shaking events of Good Friday, we are left with Holy Saturday, a day of quiet, of waiting, of grief. The body of Jesus is placed in a tomb, and the world is left in a moment of stillness. His followers, confused and heartbroken, are unsure of what to do next. The promise of resurrection is still hidden, and the silence is deafening. This is the liminal space, the in-between time, where questions remain unanswered, and hope seems sealed in the cold darkness of the tomb.

Holy Saturday invites us to sit in this silence, to acknowledge the grief and the waiting. It's a day that reminds us that not all moments of faith are filled with victory, triumph, or answers. Sometimes, we are called to wait in the quiet places, to sit with our sorrow, to reflect on our losses, and to honor the ache of unanswered prayers. Just as Jesus' disciples waited in confusion and despair, we too find ourselves in seasons of waiting, where the promises of God seem distant, and the road ahead is unclear.

But buried does not mean forgotten. Even though the body of Jesus lay in the tomb, God was still working, preparing for the greatest miracle of all. In the silence of Holy Saturday, God was orchestrating the resurrection that would change everything. What appeared to be the end was, in fact, the beginning of something greater than anyone could have imagined.

In the same way, your season of waiting, your grief, and your uncertainty do not mean that God is absent or that His promises have failed. He is still at work, even when you cannot see it. Sometimes, the silence is where God is shaping and refining us, preparing us for the resurrection to come. Even when our hope feels buried, we are never abandoned. The story isn't over, resurrection is near.

Honor the grief. Sit in the in-between. It's okay to feel the weight of loss, to wrestle with doubts, and to question what's happening. This is a holy space, one where we learn to trust God even when we don't have all the answers. You may feel like your hope is sealed in a tomb, but just as Christ was raised, so too will our hope rise again. Wait with trust, knowing that God is at work in the silence, preparing for a resurrection that will bring new life, new hope, and a renewed sense of purpose. Your waiting is not wasted; it is part of the journey toward the fullness of life in Christ.

Pause and Practice:
Sit in stillness for five minutes. Let the silence speak. Whisper, Even here, I believe.

Listen: "O Love That Will Not Let Me Go"

Day 40 - Risen

Scripture: Luke 24:6 – *"He is not here; he has risen!"*

Reflection:

Easter morning breaks through with glory, shining the light of hope into the darkest corners of our world. The tomb is empty, and the sound of victory reverberates through time: **"He has risen!"** This declaration is not just about a historical event; it is the foundation of our faith, the turning point of history. Death is defeated. The grave has lost its power. Hope is no longer a distant wish; it is a living reality. The resurrection of Jesus is the triumph of life over death, of light over darkness, of hope over despair.

But the resurrection is not just an event in the past; it is a promise for the present and the future. Because He lives, we live. Because Jesus overcame death, we too are promised victory over all that seeks to steal, kill, and destroy in our lives. The resurrection gives us a new identity, a new purpose, and a new hope. It transforms not only the world around us but also the world within us. We are raised with Christ, alive, forgiven, and empowered to live a life of purpose, love, and joy.

Easter is not the end of Lent; it is the beginning of new life. While Lent is a season of repentance, reflection, and sacrifice, Easter ushers us into the reality of resurrection. It's a moment to celebrate not just what Jesus has done, but what He continues to do in our lives. The resurrection reminds us that no matter how long the night of sorrow may last, joy comes in the morning. No matter how heavy our burdens may feel, the power of the resurrection gives us the strength to rise again.

Today, celebrate the resurrection as the beginning of new life. Just as Christ rose from the dead, you are invited to rise with Him, leaving behind the chains of sin, shame, and fear. The same power that raised Jesus from the dead lives in you. It empowers you to walk in freedom, to live with purpose, and to face the challenges of life with the confidence that Christ is with you, guiding you, and strengthening you every step of the way.

Go forward today in joy and power. This is not just a time to reflect on what Jesus did 2,000 years ago, but a moment to recognize that His resurrection power is at work in you right now. The story of Easter is not just His story; it is your story. You have been raised with Christ. You are alive in Him, and because He lives, you can face tomorrow with hope, with courage, and with the assurance that no matter what comes your way, resurrection is always possible. Let this truth fill you with joy and let that joy be the fuel that propels you into a new season of life, full of the power and presence of the risen Christ.

Pause and Practice:
Proclaim: 'He is risen indeed!' Let resurrection joy rise in you. Live as one made new.

Listen: "Christ the Lord Is Risen Today"

Benediction:
A Sending Prayer

May the One who called you into the wilderness walk with you into the resurrection.

May your ashes become beauty,
Your sorrow becomes song,
Your fasting turns to fullness,
And your wandering leads you home.

Go forth with a heart made tender,
A spirit made strong,
And a soul awakened to grace.

You have returned.
Now go and live as one who is loved.

In the name of the Father, the Son, and the Holy Spirit. Amen.

Made in the USA
Coppell, TX
08 March 2026

73439940R00059